Word Study in Action

Words Their Way

Teacher Resource Guide Ⓐ

Donald R. Bear • Marcia Invernizzi • Francine Johnston

CELEBRATION PRESS

Pearson Learning Group

Contents

Program Overview 4

   Program Components 6

   Developmental Stages...8

   Scope and Sequence 10

   Research Base 12

Using Words Their Way in Your Literacy Block 13

   How to Group Children..14

   Walk Through the Week..16

   Meeting Individual Differences.............................18

   Progress Monitoring and Using the Spell Checks 19

Lesson Plans for Level A

Week 1   Sorts 1 and 2: Beginning Consonants
b, m, r, s, t, g, n, p 20

Week 2   Sorts 3 and 4: Beginning Consonants
c, h, f, d, l, k, j, w.......................................22

Week 3   Sort 5: Beginning Consonants **y, z, v** 24

Week 4   Sort 6: Word Families **-at, -an**..............................26

Week 5   Sort 7: Word Families **-ad, -ap, -ag**.....................28

Week 6   Sort 8: Word Families **-op, -ot, -og**.....................30

Week 7   Sort 9: Word Families **-et, -eg, -en**.....................32

Week 8   Sort 10: Word Families **-ug, -ut, -un**...................34

Week 9   Sort 11: Word Families **-ip, -ig, -ill**.....................36

Week 10 Sort 12: Consonant Digraphs **ch, sh** 38

Week 11 Sort 13: Consonant Digraphs **th, wh** 40

Week 12 Sort 14: Consonant Digraphs **sh, ch, wh, th**........42

Week 13 Sort 15: Beginning Consonants and Blends
s, t, st 44

Week 14 Sort 16: Consonant Blends **sp, sk, sm**...............46

Week 15 Sort 17: Consonant Blends **sc, sn, sw** 48

Week 16 Sort 18: Consonant Blends **pl, sl, bl, fl**...............50

Week 17 Sort 19: Consonant Blends **cr, cl, fr, gl, gr**...........52

Week 18   Sort 20: Consonant Blends **pr, tr, dr, br** 54

Week 19   Sort 21: Beginning Sounds **k, wh, qu, tw** 56

Week 20   Sort 22: Word Families **-at, -ot, -it**......................58

Week 21   Sort 23: Word Families **-an, -un, -in** 60

Week 22   Sort 24: Word Families **-ad, -ed, -ab, -ob** 62

Week 23   Sort 25: Word Families **-ag, -eg, -ig, -og, -ug** 64

Week 24   Sort 26: Word Families **-ill, -ell, -all** 66

Week 25   Sort 27: Word Families **-ick, -ack, -uck, -ock**.......68

Week 26   Sort 28: Word Families **-ish, -ash, -ush** 70

Week 27   Sort 29: Short Vowels **a, o**................................72

Week 28   Sort 30: Short Vowels **i, u** 74

Week 29   Sort 31: Short Vowels **e, i, o, u**...........................76

Week 30   Sort 32: Words With Beginning Consonant Digraphs and Short Vowels **a, e, i**......................78

Week 31   Sort 33: Short Vowel Words With Beginning Blends 80

Week 32   Sort 34: Short Vowel Words With Final Blends 82

Week 33   Sort 35: Short Vowels **a, e, i, o, u** 84

Week 34   Sort 36: Long Vowels **a, i** 86

Week 35   Sort 37: Long Vowels **e, o, u** 88

Week 36   Sort 38: Long Vowels **a, e, i, o, u** 90

Program Reviewers

Pam Brown, Teacher
Sayre School
Lexington, KY

Katrina Currier, Language Arts Curriculum Coordinator
San Francisco Day School
San Francisco, CA

Kathy Lamkin, Teacher
Tuscan Elementary School
Maplewood, NJ

Shellie Winter, Teacher
Ponce de Leon Elementary School
Clearwater, FL

The following people have contributed to the development of this product:
Art and Design: Tricia Battipede, Sherri Hieber-Day, Dorothea Fox, Denise Ingrassia, David Mager, Judy Mahoney, Elbaliz Mendez
Editorial: Leslie Feierstone-Barna, Linette Mathewson, Tracey Randinelli
Inventory: Yvette Higgins
Marketing: Christine Fleming
Production/Manufacturing: Alan Dalgleish
Publishing Operations: Jennifer Van Der Heide

ISBN 0-7652-6748-9

Printed in the United States of America
3 4 5 6 7 8 9 10   08 07 06 05

Celebration Press
Pearson Learning Group

1-800-321-3106
www.pearsonlearning.com

Program Overview

Teachers have been using a *Words Their Way: Word Study for Phonics, Vocabulary, and Spelling Instruction* (Merrill/Prentice Hall, 1996, 2000, 2004), authored by noted researchers Donald R. Bear, Marcia Invernizzi, Francine Johnston, and Shane Templeton, to teach children phonics, spelling, and vocabulary, for the past eight years. This powerful approach to word study teaches children to look closely at words to discover the regularities and conventions of English orthography needed to read and spell. The success of this instruction has led Pearson Learning Group to publish *Words Their Way: Word Study in Action*, the official companion, in a ready-to-use format. This multi-component curriculum helps children increase their knowledge of the spelling patterns and the meanings of specific words and to generalize this knowledge to the English spelling system.

How Does Words Their Way: Word Study in Action Work?

The heart of the *Words Their Way: Word Study in Action* program is the **sort**, or the process of grouping sounds, words, and pictures that represent words into specific categories. Word sorting includes teacher-directed instruction as well as independent learning. You begin by demonstrating how to sort picture or word cards by sound or pattern. Later, as children sort word cards or picture cards on their own, they make discoveries and generalizations about the conventions of English orthography. They compare and contrast word features and discover similarities and differences within the categories.

Words Their Way: Word Study in Action consists of 36 sorts in Levels K, B, and C, and 38 sorts in Level A. Each sort is designed to be completed in a week. The sequence of the program is based on the alphabet, pattern, and meaning principles that have been

observed in children's spelling. *Words Their Way: Word Study in Action* provides the following important hands-on experiences:

- Comparing and contrasting words by sound so that children can categorize similar sounds and associate them consistently with letters and letter combinations. For example, words spelled with -*at* (*rat, sat, fat*) are compared with words spelled with -*ot* (*not, lot, rot*).
- Comparing and contrasting words by consistent spelling patterns associated with categories of sound. For example, words spelled with -*oi* (*join, soil, coin*) are compared with words spelled with -*oy* (*joy, annoy, coy*).
- Categorizing words by meaning, use, and parts of speech

Words Their Way: Word Study in Action and "Reading First"

In April 2000, the National Reading Panel (NRP) issued a report describing how children learn to read. As an offshoot of that report, and as part of No Child Left Behind (NCLB), the Reading First (RF) initiative was established. Reading First focuses on five areas of reading instruction needed to successfully teach children to read—phonemic awareness, phonics, fluency, comprehension, and vocabulary. Words Their Way: Word Study in Action addresses these five essential reading components in the following ways:

Phonemic awareness: Children identify picture names that begin with the same sound, isolate and say the first sound in picture names, identify and categorize rhyming words, and build words by substituting consonant and consonant blend sounds and blending them with various word families.

Phonics: Children sort pictures and/or words by initial sounds, ending sounds, consonant blends or digraphs, word families, and vowel sounds. They learn to analyze letter-sound relationships and how to identify words in word families.

Fluency: Children listen as you model fluent reading of poems from the Big Book of Rhymes, and read books from the *Words Their Way* Library that contain a variety of the phonics elements they are learning.

Comprehension: Children learn to read words quickly and accurately through word study so they are empowered to read with greater understanding.

Vocabulary: Children learn the meanings of words by sorting them according to categories, such as big things and little things or words that name things and words that name actions.

About the Authors

Donald R. Bear is director of the E. L. Cord Foundation for Learning and Literacy in the College of Education at the University of Nevada, Reno. He is a former preschool and elementary teacher whose recent research includes the study of literacy development in different languages. He currently works with many schools and districts to conduct literacy instruction workshops.

Marcia Invernizzi is a professor of reading education at the Curry School of Education at the University of Virginia. She is also the director of the McGuffey Reading Center, where she teaches the clinical practice in reading diagnosis and remedial reading. She is formerly an English and reading teacher and currently works with Phonological Awareness Literacy Screening (PALS).

Francine Johnston is an associate professor at the School of Education at the University of North Carolina at Greensboro, where she teaches courses in reading, language arts, and children's literature. Her research interests include the relationship between spelling and reading achievement.

Program Components

Words Their Way: Word Study in Action supports the routines established in *Words Their Way: Word Study for Phonics, Vocabulary, and Spelling Instruction* by providing the materials you need for each sort in a ready-to-use format. Picture and word cards, sorting grids, game boards, and reading materials that contain the same spelling patterns and vocabulary they sorted are all provided.

Words Their Way: Word Study in Action contains the following components:

Each level of the program (K, A, B, C) features a consumable **Word Study Notebook**. The Word Study Notebook contains a four-page lesson for each sort, including picture and/or word cards for children to cut out and a grid onto which children sort and paste the picture/word cards. Each lesson also contains a written activity that gives children practice in the skill that corresponds to the lesson's sort. The letter to families on the inside front cover of the Word Study Notebook connects classroom word study work with practice at home, promoting family involvement. An **envelope** is provided for children to store their picture/word cards for the week. A convenient self-stick strip allows the envelope to be attached to the inside back cover of the Word Study Notebook.

The **Big Book of Rhymes**, included with Levels K, A, and B of *Words Their Way: Word Study in Action*, contains a poem for each lesson. Words in the poems reflect the skill covered in the corresponding sort. High-interest, engaging illustrations accompany each poem and can be used to foster discussion.

All four levels of *Words Their Way: Word Study in Action* feature a **Teacher Resource Guide**, containing lesson plans for each sort in the level, along with an explanation of how to use the program and tips for progress monitoring and classroom management.

The **Teacher Resource CD** is an interactive resource provided with all four levels of *Words Their Way: Word Study in Action*. The CD-ROM contains a variety of materials that can be printed and integrated into classroom word study instruction:

- **Picture/word cards** can be used to demonstrate each sort in a level.

- **Games and activities** give children additional practice in each week's sort skill.

- **Build, Blend, and Extend activities** in levels K and A focus on building new words and blending word parts for additional phonics, phonemic awareness, and word study practice.

- **Sorts** from the last half of the previous level and the first half of the next level help you address the needs of children who may require extra practice or who may be ready for more challenging material.

- **Blank templates** allow you and your students to create your own sorts and games.

Most sorts in Levels K, A, B, and C are aligned to corresponding little books from the ***Words Their Way* Library.** Each book features a skill covered in the week's sort. Stories are age-appropriate and appealing.

An optional **storage box** with labeled file folders lets you organize all of the materials for each sort, as well as your copy of the Word Study Notebook and the Teacher Resource Guide.

Developmental Stages

Research shows that as children learn how to spell, they progress through several developmental stages of word knowledge. Levels K, A, B, and C of *Words Their Way: Word Study in Action* cover four spelling stages: Emergent, Letter Name-Alphabetic, Within Word Pattern, and Syllables and Affixes.

Emergent Spelling (Kindergarten/Level K)

During this stage, children learn to recognize and write the letters of the alphabet. They play with the sounds in words and letters. Most of the sound play focuses on beginning and rhyming sounds. Through most of Level K, children sort pictures by rhyme and beginning sounds. By the end of the level, children acquire an understanding of the concept of words, and begin to match picture cards to the words that represent their names.

Letter Name-Alphabetic Spelling (Grade 1/Level A)

At the beginning of this stage, children apply the alphabet principles primarily to consonants. By the end of the stage, children are able to represent most short vowel patterns, consonant digraphs, and consonant blends correctly. In Level A, children sort pictures and/or words by beginning consonants, digraphs, and blends, and by word families.

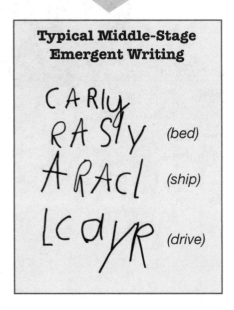

Typical Middle-Stage Emergent Writing

CARly
RASly (bed)
ARAcl (ship)
LCdyR (drive)

Typical Middle-Stage Letter Name-Alphabetic Spelling

BAD for *bed*
SEP or SHP for *ship*
FOT for *float*
LOP for *lump*

Examples	Emergent (Level K)
bed	
ship	
float	
train	
cattle	
cellar	

Within Word Pattern Spelling (Grade 2/ Level B) Children at the beginning of this stage spell most single-syllable, short vowel words correctly. Then children move away from the sound-by-sound approach of the letter name and begin to include patterns or chunks of letter sequences that relate to sound and meaning. In Level B, children begin to sort words by long vowel patterns.

Syllables and Affixes Spelling (Grade 3/ Level C) By this stage, children already spell most one-syllable short and long vowel words correctly. The focus of instruction shifts to multisyllabic words and patterns. In *Words Their Way: Word Study in Action*, children sort Level C words by specific vowel combinations, inflected endings (including plurals, -ing, and -ed), and vowel patterns in accented syllables.

Typical Middle-Stage Within Word Pattern Spelling
SPOLE for *spoil*   DRIEV for *drive*

Typical Middle-Stage Syllables and Affixes Spelling
SELLER for *cellar*   DAMIGE for *damage*   FORTUNET for *fortunate*

Stages of Spelling in *Words Their Way*

Letter Name-Alphabetic (Level A)					Within Word Pattern (Level B)				Syllables and Affixes (Level C)			
b bd	bad				bed							
s sp	sep	shep			ship							
f ft	fot	flot	flott		flowt	floaut	flote	float				
t trn	jran	tan	chran	tran	teran	traen	trane	train				
c kd	catl		cadol			catel	catol		cattel	cattle		
s slr	salr		celr			saler	celer		seler	celler	seller	cellar

Scope and Sequence

The following chart shows the skills presented in *Words Their Way: Word Study in Action*. The first column lists the skills. The subsequent columns indicate the *Words Their Way* level or levels at which the skills are covered.

Skill	Level K	Level A	Level B	Level C
Concept Sorts	•			
Rhyming Sorts	•			
Concepts of Word in Print	•			
Letter Recognition	•			
Beginning Sounds	•			
Ending Sounds **t, x**	•			
Short Vowels **a, e, i, o, u**	•	•	•	
Short Vowel Word Families	•	•		
Beginning Consonants		•		
Consonant Digraphs		•	•	
Consonant Blends		•	•	
Beginning Sounds **k, wh, qu, tw**		•		
Short Vowel Words With Beginning Consonant Digraphs		•		
Short Vowel Words With Beginning Blends		•		
Short Vowel Words With Final Blends		•		
Long Vowels **a, e, i, o, u**		•	•	
Final /k/ Sound Spelled **-ck, -ke,** or **-k**			•	
Consonant Digraphs With Short Vowels			•	
Consonant Digraphs With Long Vowels			•	
Consonant Digraphs Plus **r**-Blends and **squ**			•	
CVVC Patterns **ai, oa, ee, ea**			•	

Skill	Level K	Level A	Level B	Level C
Diphthongs			•	•
Ambiguous Vowel Sounds			•	•
Long Vowel Patterns			•	•
r-Influenced Vowel Patterns			•	•
Silent Beginning Consonants **kn, wr, gn**			•	
Triple **r**-blends **scr, str, spr**			•	•
Vowel Digraphs			•	
Hard and Soft **c** and **g**			•	•
Word Endings **-ce, -ve, -se**			•	•
Word Endings **-dge,-ge**				•
Word Endings **-tch,-ch**				•
Homophones				•
Contractions				•
Plural Endings				•
Inflected Endings: **-ing**				•
Inflected Endings: **-ed**				•
Unusual Past Tense Words				•
Compound Words				•
Syllable Juncture				•
Open and Closed Syllables and Inflected Endings				•
Long Vowel Patterns in Accented Syllables				•

Research Base

With purposeful reading, writing, listening, and speaking, words are learned. Even more words are acquired when they are explicitly examined to discover relationships among sounds, spelling patterns, and meanings.

Words Their Way: Word Study in Action increases knowledge of the spelling patterns and the meaning of specific words. Children learn to compare, contrast, and classify categories of sounds and words.

Research	Findings	Put Into Action With *Words Their Way*
Read, 1971, 1977	• Invented spellings reveal systematic, phonetic logic underlying preschoolers' categorization of English speech sounds.	• Sorts focus on discovering similarities and differences in sounds, letters, letter-sounds, words, and meaning
Henderson, Estes, & Stonecash, 1972; Beers & Henderson, 1977; Gentry, 1980; Henderson, 1981	• Invented spellings of primary school children reveal similar use of letter-name, alphabetic logic up to the next period of transition.	• Learning builds on what children know and what they are trying to negotiate.
Schlagal, 1982, 1986; Henderson & Templeton, 1986; Henderson, 1990; Invernizzi, Abouzeid & Gill, 1994	• Development study of spelling in grades one through six reveals three discernable phases of orthographic understandings: alphabet, pattern, and meaning.	• Word study progresses through systematic instruction in sound, alphabetic letter-sound correspondences, spelling patterns, and spelling-meaning connections.
Morris & Perney, 1984; Bear, Truex, & Barone, 1989; Ganske, 1999	• Developmental spelling analyses in the fall of the school year are reliable and valid predictors of literacy proficiency at the end of the school year.	• *Words Their Way* assessments place students in appropriate position in scope and sequence of *Words Their Way: Word Study in Action.*
Weber & Henderson, 1989; Hayes, 2004	• Fourth grade students assigned to word sort group significantly outperform control group on standardized measures of reading and spelling.	• Students learn to recognize, decode, and write spelling patterns.
Zutell & Rasinski, 1989; Johnston, 1998; Bear, 1992; Invernizzi, 1992; Templeton & Bear, 1992	• Orthographic knowledge significantly predicts sight word acquisition, word recognition, and oral reading fluency. Relationships among spelling, reading, and writing are reciprocal and symbiotic.	• Students categorize words by sound, pattern, and meaning, then search for other words that work the same way in poems from the Big Book of Rhymes and books from the *Words Their Way* library.
Worthy & Invernizzi, 1989; Sawyer, Lipa-Wade, Kim, Ritenour, & Knight, 1997; Cantrell, 1990, 1999; Bear, Templeton, Helman, & Baren, 2003	• Children who have learning disabilities, speak nonstandard dialects, or are learning to read in different alphabetic languages demonstrate the same types of confusions.	• Alternate sorting activities and vocabulary building, alerts and instructions for English language learners, and teacher tips are provided with each week's work so the skills can be clarified, practiced, and extended.
Morris, Blanton, Blanton, Nowacek, & Perney, 1995; Hayes, 2004	• Teaching low achieving spellers at their "instructional levels" yields greater gains than control group students who received grade-level instruction regardless of their instructional level.	• Ongoing spell checks allow for flexible grouping and differentiated phonics, spelling, and vocabulary instruction.
Templeton & Morris, 2001; Invernizzi & Hayes, 2004	• Effective word study instruction reveals the historical structures inherent in English orthography.	• Sorts and lessons focus on the systematic progression of alphabet, pattern, and meaning.

Using Words Their Way In Your Literacy Block

Words Their Way: Word Study in Action can be used in conjunction with other reading, spelling, and vocabulary programs in your classroom. Introductory lessons may take about 20 minutes, but subsequent activities should last only about 10 to 15 minutes a day and do not require much supervision. Word study can fit easily into many parts of the day.

Options for Using Words Their Way

Words Their Way: Word Study in Action can be used in a variety of classroom environments.

- **Guided reading:** If you use a guided reading program, *Words Their Way: Word Study in Action* is an excellent way to incorporate phonics into the curriculum.

- **Basal reading:** If you use a basal reading program, *Words Their Way: Word Study in Action* is an effective supplemental phonics resource that can be matched to the phonics skills you are teaching.

- **Stand-alone**: *Words Their Way: Word Study in Action* can also be used as a stand-alone spelling program.

Getting Started

One of the benefits of the *Words Their Way: Word Study in Action* program is that all of the components you need for a week's worth of instruction are easily accessible. As you begin each week, mark the pages that correspond to the week's sort in your copy of the Word Study Notebook and in the Big Book of Rhymes. Set aside copies of the little book title from the *Words Their Way* Library you'll be using during the week, and print out the picture/word cards; game; Build, Blend, and Extend activity (if applicable); and any other materials you'll need. You may find it helpful to use file folders labeled with the different sort numbers to organize your instructional materials. A file folder is also ideal to use as a base for a game board; simply attach the two game board halves to an open file folder.

Decide where children will work. Space is needed for group work, individual work, and partner work. Separate areas on the floor or at tables in one part of the classroom to work with groups as they sort and discuss their results. Encourage other children to continue to work at their desk or in other areas of the room.

How to Group Children

Words Their Way: Word Study in Action is designed to be used with small groups of approximately five to ten children. Many teachers organize three or four small groups by instructional level for reading. Word-study groups can be incorporated in these small-group reading levels.

One easy way to group students is by their proficiency within a specific level. Let's take a look at the characteristics of children at the early, middle, and late stage of each *Words Their Way: Word Study in Action* level:

Early Stage

- **Level K** Children hold the writing implement and can write on the page.
- **Level A** Children apply the alphabetic principle primarily to consonants. Sometimes strong vowels draw children's attention. For example, the long vowel at the beginning of *ice* may lead a child to spell *ice* as I or IS.
- **Level B** Children recognize initial and final consonants, consonant blends and digraphs, regular short vowel patterns, and some *r*-influenced single-syllable short vowel words.
- **Level C** Children recognize initial and final consonants, consonant blends and digraphs, short vowel patterns, most long vowel patterns, and -*ed* and most inflections.

- **Level B** Children recognize slightly more than half of the long vowel words in single-syllable words, such as *hike* and *nail*.
- **Level C** Children understand consonant doubling in words such as *shopping* and *cattle,* and doubling and *e* drop in *stopping* and *amazing.*

Middle Stage

- **Level K** Children make a clear distinction between writing and drawing. They use lines and dots for writing and create letter-like forms.
- **Level A** Children continue to focus on the letter-sound matches. They have also learned to segment and represent the middle vowel sound within words, and might spell *baker* as BAKR.

Late Stage

- **Level K** Children can make some letter-sound matches.
- **Level A** Children represent beginning, middle, and ending sounds within words, but they also learn to deal with more ambiguous sounds. Children make the match between short vowel sounds and the standard or correct short vowel spellings.
- **Level B** Children identify single-syllable long vowel words and may know some common Latin suffixes (*inspection*).
- **Level C** Children recognize long-vowel patterns in accented syllables (*compose/composition*) and some double and *e* drop words.

How do you determine which level—early, middle, or late—
your students fall into? One way is to observe what they are
using but confusing in their writing. The following chart will
help you decide where to place each child.

	Early	**Middle**	**Late**
Level K	• Drawing and scribbling for writing	• Letters, numbers, and letter-like forms • Writing may wrap from right to left at the end of a line	• Substitutions of letters that sound, feel, and look alike: *B/p, D/b*
Level A	• Letters based on point of articulation: J, JRF for *drive* • Often long vowels by letter name	• Substitutions of letter name closest in point of articulation for short vowels • Some consonant blends and digraphs	• Substitutions of common patterns for low frequency short vowels: COT for *caught*
Level B	• Long vowel markers: SNAIK for *snake*, FELE for *feel*	• Long vowel markers: NITE for *night* • Consonant patterns: SMOCK for *smoke* • Inventive substitutions in frequent, unstressed syllable patterns: TEACHAUR for *teacher* • *-ed* and other common inflections: MARCHT for *marched*, BATID for *batted*	• Low frequency long vowel words: HIEGHT for *height* • *-ed* and other common inflections • Common Latin suffixes are spelled phonetically: ATENSHUN for *attention*
Level C	• Consonant doubling: HOPING for *hopping* • Long vowel patterns in accented syllable: PERAIDING or PERADDING for *parading* • Reduced vowel in unaccented syllable: CIRCUL for *circle* • Doubling and *e* drop: AMAZZING for *amazing*	• Some silent letters: EMFASIZE for *emphasize,* INDITEMENT for *indictment*	• Some suffixes and prefixes: ATTENSION for *attention,* PERTEND for *pretend* • Vowel alternation in derivationally related pairs: COMPUSITION for *composition* • Consonant alternations in derivationally related pairs: SPACIAL for *spatial*

Walk Through the Week

The **pictures and words** in the lesson are clearly identified.

Many lessons include additional **Challenge Words** that coordinate with the skills in the lesson, for additional practice that is a bit more challenging.

The lesson plan for each sort is presented in a logical and easy-to-follow way. It provides additional ideas for sorting, building vocabulary, helping English language learners, and using challenge words.

Objectives identify the skill covered and describe what children accomplish in the lesson.

A list of **Materials** lets you see at a glance where to find each component used in the lesson.

Sort 8 — Word Families -op, -ot, -og

Objectives

- To identify short o rhyming words
- To identify and sort pictures and words with -op, -ot, or -og

Materials

 Big Book of Rhymes, Level A, "One Hot Day," page 15

 Teacher Resource CD, Level A

Word Study Notebook, Level A, pages 31–34

Words Their Way Library, Level A, *Lost in the Fog*

Teacher Resource CD, Level A, Rock Hop Game

Pictures/Words

-op	-ot	-og
mop	pot	frog
hop	dot	hog
top	hot	log
pop	cot	jog

Challenge Words

chop	slot	bog
plop	spot	cog
flop	plot	clog
shop	trot	

Day 1 — Introduce the Sort

Whole Group

Read a Rhyme: "One Hot Day"

Introduce short o rhyming words by reading the poem "One Hot Day." As you read, emphasize the words that rhyme *(spot, hot; do, too)*. As children find the rhyming words in the poem, write them in a column on the chalkboard or on chart paper. Help children understand that these words rhyme because they end with the same sound and letters. Read the poem again, omitting the last word of each line, and have children supply the missing word.

Introduce Picture/Word Sort -op, -ot, -og

Print and cut apart the picture/word cards for Sort 8 from the Teacher Resource CD. Introduce the pictures and words, defining in context any words that are unfamiliar, such as *top, cot, hog,* and *jog*. Then demonstrate for children how to sort the pictures into -op, -ot, and -og word families. Ask children to describe how the pictures in each column are alike. *(They rhyme.)* Then introduce the word cards, and ask children to match each word card to its picture.

30

Day 2 — Practice the Sort

Whole Group/Independent

You may want to begin Days 2–5 by rereading the rhyme from Day 1. Then review the previous day's sort demonstration. Help children tear out page 31 from their Word Study Notebook and cut apart the cards.

Have children work independently or with a partner to sort the picture cards by ending sound, and then match the words and pictures in each word family. Have children say the names of the pictures and read the words as they work.

Alternative Sort: Identify My Category

When children are comfortable with this week's sort, re-sort the pictures or words into groups of living and nonliving things. Begin by sorting two or three of the pictures into the categories. When you pick up the next picture or word card, invite children to identify where it will go. Continue to do this until all the cards have been sorted and children are able to identify the categories.

Day 1 — Introduce the Sort

In Levels K, A, and B, children listen as you read aloud a poem from the Big Book of Rhymes. They identify and discuss words in the poem that correspond to the lesson's skill. In the second half of the day's word study session, you use the picture/word cards located on the Teacher Resource CD to model how to perform the week's sort.

Day 2 — Practice the Sort

Review the sort with children and direct them to cut apart the picture/word cards in their Word Study Notebook. Children then sort their cards according to specific categories that reflect the sort skill.

An **Alternative Sort** provides another way for children to sort their picture/word cards.

Day 3 Find Words in Context

A corresponding book from the *Words Their Way* Library provides opportunities for both shared and independent reading, as children identify words from the text that reflect the target skill.

Day 4 Apply the Skill

Children demonstrate what they have learned by completing a writing activity found in the Word Study Notebook.

Day 3 Find Words in Context
Whole Group/Independent/Partner

Have children re-sort their cards. Then read *Lost in the Fog* with children. Have children listen for and identify any words that end with *-op*, *-ot*, or *-og*.

Have children look through their word cards to find words that match words in the text. Then have them read the story independently and find other words in the story that end with *-op*, *-ot*, or *-og*.

Day 4 Apply the Skill
Independent/Partner

Have children sort their cards again. Then have children turn to page 34 in their Word Study Notebook. Read aloud the directions, and encourage children work independently or with a partner to write words that end with *-og*, *-ot*, or *-op*.

Day 5 Complete the Sort
Whole Group/Independent

Paste in Place

Encourage children to sort and match their pictures and words into *-op*, *-ot*, and *-og* word families. Then have them turn to page 33 in their Word Study Notebook and paste the pictures and matching words in the correct column for each word family.

Play the Game

When children are finished, they may play the Rock Hop game. (See the Teacher Resource CD for the game board, playing cards, and directions.)

Building Vocabulary

If children are unfamiliar with the word *jog*, explain that it means "to run at a slow, steady pace." Invite children to stand up and practice jogging in place.

ESL/ELL English Language Learners

Review the pictures and words with children. You may need to explain that a *hog* is similar to a *pig*, that a *cot* is a small bed, and that *jog* is the same as *run*. Have children pronounce each word to be sure they are differentiating among the three endings *-op*, *-ot*, and *-og*.

Challenge Words Activity

Ask children to find other words that end with *-op*, *-ot*, or *-og*. (If children need prompting, make suggestions from the Challenge Words list on the facing page.) Then have children make word cards for these new words. They can work in small groups to sort the words into categories.

Teacher Tip

During a second or repeated sort, do not correct children when they place a picture or word in the wrong column. Wait until they have completed the sort, and have them read the words in each column to check them. If they still don't find the misplaced picture or word, tell them which column it is in, and have them find it.

You may wish to use the Sort 8 **Build, Blend, and Extend**. (See the Teacher Resource CD.)

31

Building Vocabulary

provides meanings for unfamiliar words and pictures and suggests a strategy to help children understand words they don't know.

English Language Learners

presents extra support for children through additional exploration of vocabulary in context, unfamiliar blends and vowel sounds, and other concepts that English language learners may find difficult.

Challenge Words Activity

provides a sorting activity that can be used with the Challenge Words listed on the previous page.

Teacher Tip

gives a suggestion designed to aid in areas such as instruction, assessment, and classroom management.

Day 5 Complete the Sort

Children sort their cards one final time and paste them into place on the grid in the Word Study Notebook. In the second half of the day's word study session, children play a game found on the Teacher Resource CD, such as Bingo! or Go Fish, that helps them apply the skills in the sort.

Meeting Individual Differences

Recognizing not only a child's spelling stage, but also his or her level within the stage, will help you know when to teach what. Children in Grade 1, for example, may be in the early, middle, or late level of the Letter Name-Alphabetic stage, or they may be in the late level of the previous stage (Emergent) or the early level of the next stage (Within Word Pattern).

To address this issue, sorts for the second half of the previous level and the first half of the next level are included (when applicable) on a specific level's Teacher Resource CD, ensuring that *Words Their Way: Word Study in Action* provides flexibility for all the varied instructional levels in your classroom.

In addition, you may find that your students can move through the sorts very quickly. In that case, you may wish to use more than one complete level kit in your classroom.

English Language Learners Each lesson plan in *Words Their Way: Word Study in Action* provides a suggestion for adapting the lesson to better fit the needs of English language learners. The tips cover a range of concepts that English language learners may find difficult, including letters and sounds that may be different from those in their native language, unusual spelling patterns, and vocabulary in context.

Family involvement The inside front cover of the Word Study Notebook provides an at-home activity for families to do with their children each night from Monday through Thursday.

Progress Monitoring and Using the Spell Checks

To monitor children's word-study progress, you can include a combination of writing samples, observations during oral reading, and analysis of spelling errors in formal assessments. The Spell Checks provided in each level of *Words Their Way: Word Study in Action* are another valuable assessment tool. Spell Checks are provided in the back of the Word Study Notebook. As children complete each series of skills, administer the corresponding Spell Check to determine what they have learned and what they do not understand. Then use the results of the Spell Check to plan for individual or small-group instruction.

Spell Check 1: Beginning Consonants should be used after completing Sort 5. This Spell Check assesses children's ability to identify initial consonant sounds. If children miss a beginning consonant, have them review the corresponding sort for that letter. If children miss an unusually high number of beginning consonants, they should not proceed to the next sort until they have reviewed the previous sorts.

Spell Check 2: Same Vowel Word Families should be used after completing Sort 11. This Spell Check assesses children's ability to distinguish among short vowels and recognize short vowel words. Watch for these types of errors: if you see a pattern of matching a word with the correct vowel family but the incorrect beginning sound, review Sorts 1–5 with children; if children consistently choose words from the wrong vowel family, have them review the corresponding sorts for those families.

Spell Check 3: Consonant Blends and Digraphs should be used after completing Sort 21 with children. This Spell Check assesses children's ability to identify consonant blends and digraphs used as beginning sounds. Watch for these types of errors: if you see a pattern of writing *w* for *wh*, review Sorts 13 and 21 with children; if children write *t* for *tr*, review Sort 20; if children write *f* for *fl*, review Sort 18.

Spell Check 4: Short Vowel Word Families should be used after completing Sort 28 with children. This Spell Check assesses children's ability to spell and write words containing short vowel word families. Watch for these types of errors: if children have trouble distinguishing between *a*, *i*, and *u* word families, review Sorts 23, 25, 27, and 28; if children have trouble distinguishing between *a* and *e* word families, review Sorts 24, 25, and 26.

Spell Check 5: Short Vowel Words should be used after completing Sort 35 with children. This Spell Check assesses children's ability to spell and write one-syllable short vowel words. Watch for these types of errors: if you see a pattern of writing *a* for *e* (for example, *nast* for *nest*), review Sorts 29 and 31 with children; if children write *e* for *i* (for example, *fesh* for *fish*), review Sort 31 and Sort 35.

Spell Check 6: Long Vowel Words should be used after completing Sort 38 with children. This Spell Check assesses children's ability to write one-syllable long vowel words. Watch for these types of errors: if children write *cot* for *coat*, review Sorts 37 and 38; if children write *tran* for *train* or *slid* for *slide*, review Sorts 36 or 38.

Beginning Consonants b, m, r, s, t, g, n, p

Objectives

- To recognize the beginning consonant sounds *b, m, r, s, t, g, n,* and *p*
- To sort pictures by their beginning sound and associate each sound with the letter it represents

Materials

 Big Book of Rhymes, Level A, "Go Away, Tiger!," page 5

 Teacher Resource CD, Level A

 Word Study Notebook, Level A, pages 3–10

 Words Their Way Library, Level A, *Two Boys* and *On the Farm*

 Teacher Resource CD, Level A, Concentration and Match! Games

Pictures

Bb	Mm	Rr	Ss
baby	map	rain	scissors
band	meat	ring	seal
bear	milk	road	sink
bed	monkey	rocket	six
barn	mouse	roof	soap
Tt	**Gg**	**Nn**	**Pp**
tail	game	nail	pan
tie	gate	net	peach
tire	girl	nose	pen
toe	gold	nurse	pig
tooth	goose	nut	pillow

Day 1: Introduce the Sorts

Whole Group

 Read a Rhyme: "Go Away, Tiger!"

Introduce words beginning with *b, m, r, s, t, g, n,* and *p* by reading the poem "Go Away, Tiger!" and emphasize the words that begin with each sound. Reread the poem and have children raise their hand when they hear words that begin with each targeted sound for Sorts 1 and 2 (*b, m, r, s, t, g, n, p*).

Introduce Picture Sorts
b, m, r, s, t, g, n, p

Print and cut apart the picture cards for Sorts 1 and 2 from the Teacher Resource CD. Introduce the pictures and define in context picture names that may be unfamiliar to children, such as *gold, rocket, nurse,* and *goose*. Then demonstrate for children how to name and sort the pictures belonging to Sort 1 according to beginning sound. Ask children to describe how the pictures in each column are alike. *(They begin with the same sound.)* Repeat the process with the pictures belonging to Sort 2.

Day 2: Practice the Sorts

Whole Group/Independent

 You may want to begin Days 2–5 by rereading the rhyme from Day 1. Then review the previous day's sort demonstration. Help children tear out page 3 from their Word Study Notebook and cut apart the picture cards.

Have children work independently or with a partner to say the name of each picture and, using the grid on page 5 of their Word Study Notebook, sort the cards by their beginning sounds. When they have completed Sort 1, have them repeat the process with Sort 2 on page 7 of the Word Study Notebook, using the sorting grid on page 9.

Find Words in Context

Whole Group/Independent/Partner

Have children re-sort their cards. Then read *Two Boys* with children. Have them listen for and identify any words that begin with *b, m, r,* or *s*. Then have children look through their picture cards to see if any cards match words in the text. Finally, repeat the process with *On the Farm* and the beginning sounds *t, g, n,* and *p*.

Apply the Skill

Independent/Partner

Have children sort their cards again. Then have children turn to page 6 in their Word Study Notebook. Read aloud the directions, and have children work independently or with a partner to write the letters *Bb, Mm, Rr,* and *Ss* on the lines and draw pictures of things whose names begin with those sounds. Then have children turn to page 10 in their Word Study Notebook and repeat the activity with the sounds *Tt, Gg, Nn,* and *Pp*.

Complete the Sorts

Whole Group/Independent

Paste in Place

Have children turn to page 5 in their Word Study Notebook. Encourage them to say the name of each picture and sort the cards from Sort 1 according to their beginning sound. Then have them paste the picture cards in place on the page. Finally, have them turn to page 9 of their Word Study Notebook, sort the picture cards from Sort 2, and paste them into place on the page.

Play the Game

When children are finished, they may play the Concentration and Match! games corresponding to either of the sorts covered during the week. (See the Teacher Resource CD for the playing cards and directions.)

Building Vocabulary

Show children the Sort 2 goose picture card, and ask them what other bird it looks like. Explain that a goose is a swimming bird that is like a duck but it has a larger body and longer neck.

ESL/ELL English Language Learners

Familiarize children with any unfamiliar pictures by doing a concept sort prior to sorting the pictures by beginning sound. Pictures can be sorted according to living/nonliving things, shapes, colors, and so forth.

Teacher Tip

To help children keep their Sort 1 picture cards separate from their Sort 2 cards, have them attach each sort's cards with a paper clip before storing them in the envelope found in their Word Study Notebook.

Beginning Consonants c, h, f, d, l, k, j, w

Objectives

- To recognize the beginning consonant sounds c, h, f, d, l, k, j, and w
- To sort pictures by their beginning sound and associate each sound with the letter it represents

Materials

 Big Book of Rhymes, Level A, "Time to Shop for School," page 7

 Teacher Resource CD, Level A

 Word Study Notebook, Level A, pages 11–18

 Words Their Way Library, Level A, Up They Go and For Sale

 Teacher Resource CD, Level A, Bingo! and Match! Games

Pictures

Cc	Hh	Ff	Dd
cap	ham	fan	deer
camel	hand	feather	desk
candle	hay	feet	dinosaur
cape	hen	fire	doll
carrot	hill	fish	duck
Ll	Kk	Jj	Ww
lamp	kangaroo	jacket	wagon
lid	key	jar	watch
lion	king	jeans	wave
lips	kitchen	jet	web
lizard	kitten	jump	wing

Day 1 — Introduce the Sorts

Whole Group

 Read a Rhyme: "Time to Shop for School"

Introduce words beginning with the target sounds c, h, f, d, l, k, j, and w by reading the poem "Time to Shop for School" and emphasizing the words that begin with each sound. Reread the poem and have children raise their hand when they hear words that begin with each targeted sound in Sorts 3 and 4 (c, h, f, d, l, k, j, w).

 Introduce Picture Sorts c, h, f, d, l, k, j, w

Print and cut apart the picture cards for Sorts 3 and 4 from the Teacher Resource CD. Introduce the pictures and define in context picture names that may be unfamiliar to children, such as *hay* and *cape*. Then demonstrate for children how to name and sort the pictures belonging to Sort 3. Ask children to describe how the pictures in each column are alike. Repeat the process with the pictures belonging to Sort 4.

Day 2 — Practice the Sorts

Whole Group/Independent

 You may want to begin Days 2–5 by rereading the rhyme from Day 1. Then review the previous day's sort demonstration. Help children remove page 11 from their Word Study Notebook and cut apart the picture cards.

Have children work independently or with a partner to say the name of each picture and, using the grid on page 13 of their Word Study Notebook, sort the cards by their beginning sound. When they have finished with Sort 3, have them repeat the process with Sort 4, using pages 15 and 17 of the Word Study Notebook.

Day 3

Find Words in Context

Whole Group/Independent/Partner

Have children re-sort their cards. Then read *Up They Go* with children. Have children listen for and identify any words that begin with *c, h, f,* or *d.* Then have children look through their picture cards to see if any match words in the text. Finally, repeat the process with *For Sale* and the beginning sounds *l, k, j,* and *w.*

Day 4

Apply the Skill

Independent/Partner

Have children sort their cards again. Then have children turn to page 14 in their Word Study Notebook. Read aloud the directions, and have children work independently or with a partner to write the letters *Cc, Hh, Ff,* and *Dd* on the lines and draw pictures of things whose names begin with each of those sounds. Then have children turn to page 18 and repeat the activity with the letters *Ll, Kk, Jj,* and *Ww.*

Day 5

Complete the Sorts

Whole Group/Independent

Paste in Place

Have children turn to page 13 in their Word Study Notebook. Encourage children to say the name of each picture and sort the cards from Sort 3 according to their beginning sound. Then have them paste the pictures in place on the page. Finally, have children sort the picture cards for Sort 4 on the grid on page 17 of their Word Study Notebook and paste them in place.

Play the Game

When children are finished, they may play the Bingo! and Match! games corresponding to either of the sorts covered during the week. (See the Teacher Resource CD for the game boards, playing cards, and directions.)

Building Vocabulary

If children are unfamiliar with the word *cape,* explain that it is a type of coat that doesn't have sleeves and is fastened at the neck. Discuss with children how the picture for *cape* might help them understand the word's meaning.

ESL/ELL English Language Learners

Keep in mind that the names of some of the pictures may contain sounds that do not exist in a child's native language. Guide children by asking them to repeat the name of each picture after you, as needed.

Teacher Tip

Encourage children whose names begin with a letter featured in Sort 3 or 4 to play the Bingo! game for that particular sort.

Sort 5

Beginning Consonants y, z, v

Objectives

- To identify picture names beginning with the sounds of *y, z, v*
- To sort pictures by their beginning sound and associate each sound with the letter it represents

Materials

Big Book of Rhymes, Level A, "A Day at the Zoo," page 9

Teacher Resource CD, Level A

Word Study Notebook, Level A, pages 19–22

Words Their Way Library, Level A, *Good-bye, Zoo*

Teacher Resource CD, Level A, Bingo! Game

Pictures

Yy	Zz	Vv
yo-yo	zigzag	vase
yell	zebra	vine
yard	zero	violin
yarn	zucchini	volcano
yawn	zoo	vest

Day 1 Introduce the Sort

Whole Group

Read a Rhyme: "A Day at the Zoo"

Introduce words with the target sounds *y, z,* and *v* by reading the poem "A Day at the Zoo." Reread the poem, and have children listen for words that begin like *yak, zebra,* and *van.* Have them raise their hand when they hear words that begin with the target sounds. Reread the poem until children recognize the words with the three target sounds.

Introduce Picture Sort y, z, v

Print and cut apart the picture cards for Sort 5 from the Teacher Resource CD. Introduce the pictures and define in context picture names that may be unfamiliar to children, such as *yo-yo, zigzag, zucchini,* and *violin.* Then demonstrate how to name and sort the pictures by their beginning consonant sound. Have children describe how the picture names in each column are alike. *(They begin with the same sound.)* Then have children identify which letter stands for each sound.

Day 2 Practice the Sort

Whole Group/Independent/Partner

You may want to begin Days 2–5 by rereading the rhyme from Day 1. Then review the previous day's sort demonstration. Help children tear out page 19 from their Word Study Notebook and cut apart the picture cards.

Have children work independently or with a partner to say each picture name and, using the grid on page 21 of their Word Study Notebook, sort the cards by their beginning sound.

Alternative Sort: Object or Action

When children are comfortable with this week's sort, stack the picture cards facedown. Tell children that they will sort the cards into two categories—objects and actions. Hold up the picture card of the zucchini and explain that it is an object. Then hold up the picture card for yell and explain that it is an action. Have children select a card, say its name, and place it in either the correct column. Continue until all the cards have been sorted.

Day 3 — Find Words in Context

Whole Group/Independent

Have children re-sort their cards. Then read *Good-bye, Zoo* with children. Have them listen for and identify any words that begin with the sounds of *y, z,* and *v*.

Have children look through their picture cards to find words that match the text. *(zoo, zebra, yell)* Then have them find other words in the story that begin with *z. (zip, zoom)* Help them read the words aloud.

Day 4 — Apply the Skill

Independent/Partner

Have children sort their cards again. Then have children turn to page 22 in their Word Study Notebook. Read aloud the directions. Have children work independently or with a partner to write the letters and draw pictures of things whose names begin like *yarn, zipper,* and *van.*

Day 5 — Complete the Sort

Whole Group/Independent

Paste in Place

Have children turn to page 21 in their Word Study Notebook. Encourage them to say the name of each picture and sort their cards according to their beginning sound. Then have them paste the pictures in place on the page.

Play the Game

When children are finished, they may play the Bingo! game. (See the Teacher Resource CD for the game board, playing cards and directions.)

Building Vocabulary

Using the zigzag picture card, lead children to discover that a zigzag has sharp turns, first to one side and then to the other. Ask children if they have seen lightning zigzag across the sky and where else they have seen something that zigzags. Have children demonstrate zigzag walking.

ESL/ELL English Language Learners

Review the picture names and discuss those picture names that might be unfamiliar to children, such as *violin, zucchini, zigzag,* or *volcano.* Ask children to use each word in a sentence to demonstrate their understanding.

Teacher Tip

If children experience difficulty discriminating among the consonant sounds, have them draw out the initial consonant sound as they say the name of the column heads and then each picture name.

 Spell Check 1

After completing Sorts 1–5, you may want to administer Spell Check 1 in the Word Study Notebook on page 155. See page 19 for instructions on assessment.

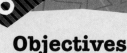

Sort 6

Word Families -at, -an

Objectives

- To identify short *a* rhyming words
- To identify and sort pictures and words with *-at* and *-an*

Materials

 Big Book of Rhymes, Level A, "The Snowman," page 11

 Teacher Resource CD, Level A

 Word Study Notebook, Level A, pages 23–26

 Words Their Way Library, Level A, *Look at That!*

 Teacher Resource CD, Level A, Word Maker Game

Pictures/Words

-at	-an
mat	can
bat	van
hat	fan
rat	man

Challenge Words

flat	ban
chat	plan
scat	scan
that	tan

Day 1 — Introduce the Sort

Whole Group

 Read a Rhyme: "The Snowman"

Introduce short *a* rhyming words by reading the poem "The Snowman." As you read, emphasize the words that rhyme. *(fat, hat; snowman, pan)* As children find the rhyming words in the poem, write them in two columns on the chalkboard or on chart paper. Then ask children how the words are alike. Help children understand that each word pair ends with the same sound and letters, and that they rhyme. Read the poem again, omitting the last word of each line, and have children provide the missing word.

 Introduce Picture/Word Sort -an, -at

Print and cut apart the picture/word cards for Sort 6 from the Teacher Resource CD. Introduce the pictures and words, and define in context words that may be unfamiliar, such as *van* and *mat*. Then demonstrate how to sort the pictures into *-at* and *-an* families. Ask children to describe how the names of the pictures in each column are alike. Then invite children to match each word to its picture.

Day 2 — Practice the Sort

Whole Group/Independent/Partner

 You may want to begin Days 2–5 by rereading the rhyme from Day 1. Then review the previous day's sort demonstration. Help children tear out page 23 from their Word Study Notebook and cut apart the cards.

Have children work independently or with a partner to say the name of each picture and, using the grid on page 25 of their Word Study Notebook, sort the picture cards by ending sound. Then have them match the words and pictures in each word family.

> ### Alternative Sort: Identify My Category
>
> Re-sort the pictures or words into groups of living and nonliving things. Begin by sorting two or three of the pictures into the categories. When you pick up the next picture or word card, invite children to identify where it will go. Continue to do this until all the cards have been sorted and children are able to identify the categories.

Day 3
Find Words in Context

Whole Group/Independent

Have children re-sort their cards. Then read *Look at That!* with children. Have children listen for and identify any words that end with -*at* or -*an*.

Have children look through their word cards to find those that match words in the *text. (fan, hat, can, bat, man)* Then have them find other words in the story that end with -*at* or -*an*. *(pan, that, at)*

Day 4
Apply the Skill

Independent/Partner

Have children sort their cards again. Then have children turn to page 26 in their Word Study Notebook. Read aloud the directions, and have children work independently or with a partner to write words that rhyme with *bat* and *can*.

Day 5
Complete the Sort

Whole Group/Independent

Paste in Place

Have children turn to page 25 in their Word Study Notebook. Encourage children to say the name of each picture and then sort their pictures and words according to -*at* and -*an* word families. Then have them paste the pictures in place on the page.

Play the Game

When children are finished, they may play the Word Maker game. (See the Teacher Resource CD for the playing cards and directions.)

Building Vocabulary

Explain that a mat can be a pad used by a door. Ask how it is different from a rug and what its purpose is. Then have children name other mats and tell why they are used. These may include place mats, exercise or sporting mats, and picture mats.

ESL/ELL English Language Learners

Review with children some words or pictures of things that end with -*an* and -*at*. Have them attend to the formation of all three sounds in each word. Have children draw out the last sound in each word to help them better hear the difference between the sounds of -*an* and -*at*.

Challenge Words Activity

Ask children to find other words that end with -*an* or -*at* in books or other texts around them. If children need prompting, make suggestions from the Challenge Words list. Then have children make word cards for the new words. They can work in pairs or small groups to use each word in a sentence and then sort the words into categories.

Teacher Tip

Invite children to make large outlines of a cat and a man for posting in the classroom. Have children write all the rhyming words they can think of inside each figure. Then read the words aloud as a group, and display the completed outlines.

You may wish to use the Sort 6 **Build, Blend, and Extend**. (See the Teacher Resource CD.)

Sort 7
Word Families -ad, -ap, -ag

Objectives

- To identify short *a* rhyming words
- To identify and sort pictures and words with -*ad*, -*ap*, and -*ag*

Materials

 Big Book of Rhymes, Level A, "Where's My Cap?," page 13

 Teacher Resource CD, Level A

 Word Study Notebook, Level A, pages 27–30

 Words Their Way Library, Level A, *Haddie's Caps*

 Teacher Resource CD, Level A, Find the Cap Game

Pictures/Words

-ad	-ap	-ag
sad	nap	rag
dad	cap	wag
pad	lap	bag

Challenge Words

lad	clap	sag
glad	flap	drag
	snap	snag

Day 1 Introduce the Sort

Whole Group

 Read a Rhyme: "Where's My Cap?,"

As you read the poem "Where's My Cap?,"
emphasize the words that rhyme *(cap, nap;
dad, bad; wag, rag)*. Reread the poem, and ask
children to find and read the rhyming words.
Write them in three columns on the chalkboard.
Then ask children how the words in each column
are alike. (They end with the same sounds and
letters and they rhyme.) Reread the poem again,
omitting the last word of each line, and have
children provide the rhyming word.

 **Introduce Picture/Word Sort -*ad*,
-*ap*, -*ag***

Print and cut apart the picture/word cards for
Sort 7 from the Teacher Resource CD. Introduce
the pictures and words, and define in context
words that may be unfamiliar to children, such
as *pad* and *wag*. Then demonstrate how to sort
the pictures into -*ad*, -*ap*, and -*ag* word families.
Ask children to describe how the names of the
pictures in each column are alike. *(They rhyme.)*
Then introduce the word cards, and invite
children to match each word to its picture.

Day 2 Practice the Sort

Whole Group/Partner/Independent

 You may want to begin Days 2–5 by rereading
the rhyme from Day 1. Then review the
previous day's sort demonstration. Help
children tear out page 27 from their Word
Study Notebook and cut apart the cards.

Have children work with a partner or
independently to say the name of each picture
and, using the grid on page 29 of their Word
Study Notebook, sort their cards by their
ending sound. Then have them match the
words and pictures in each word family.

**Alternative Sort:
Identify My Category**

When children are comfortable with this
week's sort, re-sort the pictures or words
except *sad* and *dad*. Begin sorting the cards
into the categories of actions *(nap, wag)*
and things people use or have *(rag, pad,
bag, cap, lap)*. When you pick up the next
picture or word card, invite children to
identify where it will go. Continue to do this
until all the cards have been sorted.

Day 3 — Find Words in Context

Whole Group/Independent/Partner

Have children re-sort their cards. Then read *Haddie's Caps* with children. Have children listen for and identify any words that end with *-ad*, *-ap*, or *-ag*.

Have children look through their word cards to find ones that match words in the text. *(had, cap, sad)* Then have them find and read aloud other words in the story that end with *-ad* or *-ap*. *(glad, had, mad, rap, snap)*.

Day 4 — Apply the Skill

Independent/Partner

Have children sort their cards again. Then have children turn to page 30 in their Word Study Notebook. Read aloud the directions, and have children work independently or with a partner to write words that rhyme with *sad, lap,* or *bag*.

Day 5 — Complete the Sort

Whole Group/Independent

Paste in Place

Have children turn to page 29 in their Word Study Notebook. Encourage them to sort their pictures and words according to *-ad*, *-ap*, and *-ag* word families. Then have them paste the pictures and matching words in the correct column for each word family.

Play the Game

When children are finished, they may play the Find the Cap game. (See the Teacher Resource CD for the game board, playing cards, and directions.

Building Vocabulary

Children may know and be able to name several kinds of pads different from the writing pad shown on the picture card. Have them brainstorm all the different kinds of pads, such as sports pads, computer mouse pads, launch pads, furniture pads, lily pads, and stamp or inkpads.

ESL/ELL English Language Learners

Have children work to match picture and word cards. As each match is made, model using the word in a sentence. Then have children pantomime the sentence to check for understanding.

Challenge Words Activity

Write a Challenge Word on the board, and read it aloud. Then say a rhyming word and have a child show how to change the first word, to make the second word. Repeat the process for the other word families. Then have children brainstorm *-ad*, *-ap*, and *-ag* words and write the words on cards. They can work in pairs or small groups to use each of the words in a sentence and then sort the words into categories.

Teacher Tip

If children have difficulty sorting, focus on only two word families. After children demonstrate an understanding of the two families, introduce the third family.

Word Families -op, -ot, -og

Objectives

- To identify short *o* rhyming words
- To identify and sort pictures and words with *-op, -ot,* or *-og*

Materials

 Big Book of Rhymes, Level A, "One Hot Day," page 15

 Teacher Resource CD, Level A

 Word Study Notebook, Level A, pages 31–34

 Words Their Way Library, Level A, *Lost in the Fog*

 Teacher Resource CD, Level A, Rock Hop Game

Pictures/Words

-op	-ot	-og
mop	pot	frog
hop	dot	hog
top	hot	log
pop	cot	jog

Challenge Words

chop	slot	bog
plop	spot	cog
flop	plot	clog
shop	trot	

Day 1 — Introduce the Sort

Whole Group

 Read a Rhyme: "One Hot Day"

Introduce short *o* rhyming words by reading the poem "One Hot Day." As you read, emphasize the words that rhyme *(spot, hot; do, too)*. As children find the rhyming words in the poem, write them in a column on the chalkboard or on chart paper. Help children understand that these words rhyme because they end with the same sound and letters. Read the poem again, omitting the last word of each line, and have children supply the missing word.

 Introduce Picture/Word Sort -op, -ot, -og

Print and cut apart the picture/word cards for Sort 8 from the Teacher Resource CD. Introduce the pictures and words, defining in context any words that are unfamiliar, such as *top, cot, hog,* and *jog.* Then demonstrate for children how to sort the pictures into *-op, -ot,* and *-og* word families. Ask children to describe how the pictures in each column are alike. *(They rhyme.)* Then introduce the word cards, and ask children to match each word card to its picture.

Day 2 — Practice the Sort

Whole Group/Independent

 You may want to begin Days 2–5 by rereading the rhyme from Day 1. Then review the previous day's sort demonstration. Help children tear out page 31 from their Word Study Notebook and cut apart the cards.

Have children work independently or with a partner to sort the picture cards by ending sound, and then match the words and pictures in each word family. Have children say the names of the pictures and read the words as they work.

Alternative Sort: Identify My Category

When children are comfortable with this week's sort, re-sort the pictures or words into groups of living and nonliving things. Begin by sorting two or three of the pictures into the categories. When you pick up the next picture or word card, invite children to identify where it will go. Continue to do this until all the cards have been sorted and children are able to identify the categories.

Day 3 Find Words in Context

Whole Group/Independent/Partner

Have children re-sort their cards. Then read *Lost in the Fog* with children. Have children listen for and identify any words that end with *-op, -ot,* or *-og.*

Have children look through their word cards to find words that match words in the text. Then have them read the story independently and find other words in the story that end with *-op, -ot,* or *-og.*

Day 4 Apply the Skill

Independent/Partner

Have children sort their cards again. Then have children turn to page 34 in their Word Study Notebook. Read aloud the directions, and encourage children work independently or with a partner to write words that end with *-og, -ot,* or *-op.*

Day 5 Complete the Sort

Whole Group/Independent

Paste in Place

Encourage children to sort and match their pictures and words into *-op, -ot,* and *-og* word families. Then have them turn to page 33 in their Word Study Notebook and paste the pictures and matching words in the correct column for each word family.

Play the Game

When children are finished, they may play the Rock Hop game. (See the Teacher Resource CD for the game board, playing cards, and directions.)

Building Vocabulary

If children are unfamiliar with the word *jog,* explain that it means "to run at a slow, steady pace." Invite children to stand up and practice jogging in place.

ESL/ELL English Language Learners

Review the pictures and words with children. You may need to explain that a *hog* is similar to a *pig,* that a *cot* is a small bed, and that jog is the same as run. Have children pronounce each word to be sure they are differentiating among the three endings *-op, -ot,* and *-og.*

Challenge Words Activity

Ask children to find other words that end with *-op, -ot,* or *-og.* (If children need prompting, make suggestions from the Challenge Words list on the facing page.) Then have children make word cards for these new words. They can work in small groups to sort the words into categories.

Teacher Tip

During a second or repeated sort, do not correct children when they place a picture or word in the wrong column. Wait until they have completed the sort, and have them read the words in each column to check them. If they still don't find the misplaced picture or word, tell them which column it is in, and have them find it.

You may wish to use the Sort 8 **Build, Blend, and Extend**. (See the Teacher Resource CD.)

Sort 9
Word Families -et, -eg, -en

Objectives

- To identify short e rhyming words
- To identify and sort pictures and words with -et, -eg, and -en

Materials

Big Book of Rhymes, Level A, "Ben's Red Hen," page 17

Teacher Resource CD, Level A

Word Study Notebook, Level A, pages 35–38

Words Their Way Library, Level A, *Ben's Pets*

Teacher Resource CD, Level A, Find the Hen Game

Pictures/Words

-et	-eg	-en
net	leg	pen
pet	peg	hen
jet	beg	men
wet		ten

Challenge Words

bet	Meg	Ben
let	Greg	den
set		when
fret		then

Day 1 Introduce the Sort

Whole Group

Read a Rhyme: "Ben's Red Hen"

Introduce short e rhyming words by reading the poem "Ben's Red Hen." Reread the poem and have children find the words and names that rhyme. *(Ben, hen, ten; leg, Meg; bet, met)* Write the words in three columns on the chalkboard. Help children understand that the words in each column end with the same sounds and letters, and that they rhyme. Reread the poem again, omitting the last word of each line, and have children provide the missing word.

Introduce Picture/Word Sort -et, -eg, -en

Print and cut apart the cards for Sort 9 from the Teacher Resource CD. Introduce the pictures and words, and define in context picture names that may be unfamiliar to children, such as *peg*, *beg*, and *hen*. Then demonstrate how to sort the pictures into -et, -eg, and -en word families. Ask children to describe how the names of the pictures in each column are alike. *(They rhyme.)* Then introduce the word cards, and invite children to match each word to its picture.

Day 2 Practice the Sort

Whole Group/Independent/Partner

You may want to begin Days 2–5 by rereading the rhyme from Day 1. Then review the previous day's sort demonstration. Help children tear out page 35 from their Word Study Notebook and cut apart the cards.

Have children work independently or with a partner to say each picture name and, using the grid on page 37 of their Word Study Notebook, sort the cards by ending sounds and match the words and pictures in each word family.

Alternative Sort: One and More Than One

Have children re-sort all of the pictures or words except *wet* and *beg*. Begin sorting cards into the categories of words that name one thing (*net, pet, jet, leg, peg, pen, hen*) and words that name more than one (*men, ten*). When you show the next picture or word card, invite children to identify where it will go. Continue to do this until all the cards have been sorted. Then have children read the rhyming words in each column.

Day 3 Find Words in Context

Whole Group/Independent

Have children re-sort their cards. Then read *Ben's Pets* with children. Have children listen for and identify any words that end with -*et*, -*eg*, or -*en*.

Have children look through their word cards to find the ones that match words in the text. *(pet, hen)* Then have them find other words in the story that end like *pet*. *(get, vet)*

Day 4 Apply the Skill

Independent/Partner

Have children sort their cards again. Then have children turn to page 38 in their Word Study Notebook. Read aloud the directions and have children work independently or with a partner to write write words that rhyme with *net*, *peg*, and *pen*.

Day 5 Complete the Sort

Whole Group/Independent

Paste in Place

Have children turn to page 37 in their Word Study Notebook. Encourage children to sort their pictures and words according to -*et*, -*eg*, and -*en* word families. Then have them paste the pictures and matching words in the correct column for each word family.

Play the Game

When children are finished, they may play the Find the Hen game. (See the Teacher Resource CD for the game board, playing cards, and directions.

Building Vocabulary

Clarify differences between a peg, a hook, and a nail. Show an example of each or sketch so children can tell differences. Ask where children have seen pegs being used, such as pegs for hanging clothing or cups, or for marking a score in a game.

ESL/ELL English Language Learners

If any child has difficulty recalling an English word for a picture in this sort, focus on the word at the time of confusion. Model and have all children in the group repeat several sentences about the picture, using the particular word in each sentence.

Challenge Words Activity

Ask children to find other words that end with -*et*, -*eg*, or -*en*. If children need prompting, make suggestions from the Challenge Words list on the facing page. Then have children make word cards for these new words. They can work in small groups to sort the words into categories.

Teacher Tip

Three target words can be used to focus on final sound/letter correspondence. Write *pet* on the chalkboard. Then have children show how they can change one letter to first make *peg* and then *pen*.

Word Families -ug, -ut, -un

Objectives

- To identify short *u* rhyming words
- To identify and sort pictures and words with *-ug*, *-ut*, or *-un*

Materials

 Big Book of Rhymes, Level A, "A Bug and a Nut," page 19

 Teacher Resource CD, Level A

 Word Study Notebook, Level A, pages 39–42

 Words Their Way Library, Level A, *Good Night, Little Bug*

 Teacher Resource CD, Level A, Rhyming Go Fish game

Pictures/Words

-ug	-ut	-un
bug	cut	run
rug	hut	bun
mug	nut	sun

Challenge Words

plug	strut	fun
slug	rut	spun
snug	shut	stun

Day 1 — Introduce the Sort

Whole Group

Read a Rhyme: "A Bug and a Nut"

Introduce short *u* rhyming words by reading the poem "A Bug and a Nut." Reread the poem and have children find the words that rhyme. *(sun, run, fun; bug, tug, rug)* Write the sets of rhyming words in two columns on the chalkboard or on chart paper. Then ask children how the words in each column are alike. *(They rhyme and end with the same sounds.)*

Introduce Picture/Word Sort -ug, -ut, -un

Print and cut apart the picture/word cards for Sort 10 from the Teacher Resource CD. Introduce the pictures and words, and define in context words that may be unfamiliar to children, such as *mug* and *nut*. Demonstrate for children how to sort the pictures into *-ug*, *-ut*, and *-un* word families. Then introduce the word cards, and invite children to match each word to its picture. Help children understand that the words in each column rhyme and have the same endings.

Day 2 — Practice the Sort

Whole Group/Independent/Partner

You may want to begin Days 2–5 by rereading the rhyme from Day 1. Then review the previous day's sort demonstration. Help children tear out page 39 from their Word Study Notebook and cut apart the cards.

Have children work independently or with a partner to say the name of each picture and, using the grid on page 41 in their Word Study Notebook, sort the cards by ending sound. Then have them match the words to the pictures in each word family. Encourage children to read the word cards as they work.

Alternative Sort: Compare and Contrast

Display the rhyme "A Bug and a Nut." Begin sorting two word cards into the categories of words that can be found in the rhyme and words that are not in the rhyme. As you show each word card, invite children to read it and place it in the correct category. Reread the columns together.

Day 3

Find Words in Context

Whole Group/Independent

Have children re-sort their cards. Then read *Good Night, Little Bug* with children. Have children listen for and identify any words that end with *-ug*, *-ut*, or *-un*.

Have children look through their word cards to find ones that match words in the text (*run, bug, nut*). Then have children find other words in the story that end with *-ug* or *-un*. (*hug, fun, snug*)

Day 4

Apply the Skill

Independent/Partner

Have children sort their cards again. Then have children turn to page 42 in their Word Study Notebook. Read aloud the directions, and have children work independently or with a partner to write words that rhyme with *rug, hut,* and *run*.

Day 5

Complete the Sort

Whole Group/Independent

Paste in Place

Have children turn to page 41 in their Word Study Notebook. Encourage children to sort their pictures and words according to *-ug, -ut,* and *-un* word families. Then have them paste the pictures and matching words in the correct column for each word family.

Play the Game

When children are finished, they may play the Rhyming Go Fish game. (See the Teacher Resource CD for playing cards and directions.)

Building Vocabulary

Using the *shut, cut,* and *run* picture cards, have children tell how these photographs are similar. Lead children to understand that each of these photographs shows an action rather than an object. Ask children to think of other ways these actions could be shown.

ESL/ELL English Language Learners

If children confuse the medial short vowels *e* and *u*, such as *beg* and *bug*, pair them with a proficient English speaker to work with a list of the confused words. They can make a simple book of sentences using the words and pictures for this sort. When finished, the partners can take turns tape-recording each page; this gives the English language learner opportunities to replay the tape to compare pronunciation.

Challenge Words Activity

Help children make seven letter cards: *g, l, n, p, s, t, u.* Have them show you how they can build *sun*, change it to *spun*, and then make another substitution to build *stun*. As words are built, discuss their meanings and model their usage in sentences. Repeat the process for *plug* to *slug* to *snug*.

Teacher Tip

Individual sets of letter cards made from card stock or posterboard, for a week's target words, can be easily banded together and kept in children's desks to pull out for ten-minute word-building practice.

Word Families -ip, -ig, -ill

Objectives

- To identify short *i* rhyming words
- To identify and sort pictures and words with -ip, -ig, or -ill

Materials

 Big Book of Rhymes, Level A, "Mr. Fig Met a Pig," page 21

 Teacher Resource CD, Level A

 Word Study Notebook, Level A, pages 43–46

 Words Their Way Library, Level A, *Mr. Fin's Trip*

 Teacher Resource CD, Level A, Zip Up the Hill game

Pictures/Words

-ip	-ig	-ill
zip	pig	Jill
rip	wig	sill
lip	dig	mill

Challenge Words

chip	rig	chill
slip	twig	drill
flip	jig	still
clip		spill

Day 1 — Introduce the Sort

Whole Group

 Read a Rhyme: "Mr. Fig Met a Pig"

Introduce short *i* rhyming words by reading the poem, "Mr. Fig Met a Pig." As you read, have children find and say the rhyming words. *(hill, Jill; pig, big; flip, zip)* Write the rhyming words in three columns on the chalkboard or on chart paper. Help children understand that these words rhyme because they end with the same sound and letters. Read the poem again, omitting the last word of each line, and have the children provide the missing word.

 Introduce Picture/Word Sort -ip, -ig, -ill

Print and cut apart the picture/word cards for Sort 11 from the Teacher Resource CD. Introduce the pictures and words, and define in context words that may be unfamiliar to children, such as *rip*, *sill*, and *mill*. Demonstrate for children how to sort the pictures into -ip, -ig, and -ill word families. Then introduce the word cards, and invite children to match each word to its picture. Ask children to describe how the words in each column are alike. *(They rhyme and have the same endings.)*

Day 2 — Practice the Sort

Whole Group/Independent/Partner

 You may want to begin Days 2–5 by rereading the rhyme from Day 1. Then review the previous day's sort demonstration. Help children tear out page 43 from their Word Study Notebook and cut apart the cards.

Have children work independently or with a partner to say each picture name and, using the grid on page 45 of their Word Study Notebook, sort the cards by ending sound. Then have them match the words and pictures in each word family. Encourage children to read the word cards as they work.

Alternative Sort: Object or Action

Re-sort the pictures or words into groups of actions *(zip, rip, dig)* and things *(sill, lip, mill)*. Begin by sorting two or three of the pictures into the categories. When you pick up the next picture or word card, invite children to identify where it will go. Continue until all the cards have been sorted and children are able to identify the categories.

Day 3 Find Words in Context

Whole Group/Independent

Have children re-sort their cards. Then read *Mr. Fin's Trip* with children. Have children listen for and identify any words that end with *-ip*.

Have children look through their word cards to find one that matches a word in the text *(rip)*. Then have them find other words in the story that end with *-ip*. *(ship, trip)*

Day 4 Apply the Skill

Independent/Partner

Have children sort their cards again. Then have children turn to page 46 in their Word Study Notebook. Read aloud the directions and have children work independently or with a partner to write words that rhyme with *lip, dig,* and *mill.*

Day 5 Complete the Sort

Whole Group/Independent

Paste in Place

Have children turn to page 45 in their Word Study Notebook. Encourage children to sort the pictures by their ending sound and match them to the word cards. Then have them paste the pictures and matching words in the correct column for each word family.

Play the Game

When children are finished, they may play the Zip Up the Hill game. (See the Teacher Resource CD for the game board, playing cards, and directions.)

Building Vocabulary

Ask if children know what a mill is. Explain that factory-type mills make flour or cloth but small mills are used in some homes for grinding or crushing pepper or coffee. Then show children the mill picture, and discuss which type it is.

ESL/ELL English Language Learners

Throughout the week, ensure that children hear and correctly say the middle and last sounds in the target words. Slowly repeat native speakers' sentences or spoken words, and have the group then repeat them with you.

Challenge Words Activity

List some or all of the Challenge Words. Guide children's reading of the list. Then model how they can take turns using Challenge Words as the answer to a puzzle: "I'm thinking of a word that rhymes with *hill*. It can mean "quiet." What is it?" *(still)*

Teacher Tip

Keeping a posted list of each week's word families, even after Day 5, can encourage children's ongoing comparison of new words, build recognition speed through rereading, and lead to feelings of accomplishment. Have children add to the word families as they read more texts and study across the curriculum.

You may wish to use the Sort 11 **Build, Blend, and Extend**. (See the Teacher Resource CD.)

Spell Check 2

After completing Sorts 6–11, you may want to administer Spell Check 2 in the Word Study Notebook on page 156. See page 19 for instructions on assessment.

Consonant Digraphs ch, sh

Objectives

- To identify the digraphs *ch* and *sh*
- To identify and sort pictures by beginning sounds *ch* or *sh*

Materials

 Big Book of Rhymes, Level A, "On Our Ship," page 23

 Teacher Resource CD, Level A

 Word Study Notebook, Level A, pages 47–50

 Words Their Way Library, Level A, *The Ship*

 Teacher Resource CD, Level A, Bingo! game

Pictures

ch	sh
chick	shirt
chair	shell
chimney	shoe
check	ship
chin	shadow
cheese	shelf

Challenge Words

chip	shin
chill	shot
chug	shun

Day 1 — Introduce the Sort

Whole Group

 Read a Rhyme: "On Our Ship"

Introduce words with the target sounds in readings of the poem "On Our Ship." As you read, emphasize the words *ship* and *chance*. Reread the first sentence, and have children listen for the word *ship*. Write *sh* on the chalkboard and point out that the beginning sound of *ship* is spelled with two letters. Reread the second sentence, and repeat the process for *chance*. Read the poem again, omitting the two target words, and have children provide those words.

 Introduce Picture Sort ch, sh

If you have not already done so, print and cut apart the picture cards for Sort 12 from the Teacher Resource CD. Introduce the pictures and define in context picture names that may be unfamiliar to children, such as *chimney*, *check*, and *ship*. Then demonstrate how to sort the picture names by their beginning sound. Have children describe how the names for the pictures in each column are alike and which letters make each sound.

Day 2 — Practice the Sort

Whole Group/Independent/Partner

 You may want to begin Days 2–5 by rereading the rhyme from Day 1. Then review the previous day's sort demonstration. Help children tear out page 47 from their Word Study Notebook and cut apart the cards.

Have children work independently or with a partner to say the name of each picture and, using the grid on page 49 of their Word Study Notebook, sort the cards by their beginning sound.

> **Alternative Sort: Can People Make It?**
>
> When children are comfortable with this week's sort, lead them to re-sort the pictures into two columns of categories: things that people can make (*chair, chimney, check, cheese, shirt, shelf, shoe, ship, shadow*) and things that people cannot make (*chick, chin, shell*). Ask children if they know and can pantomime how each manufactured or handmade item is created.

Day 3

Find Words in Context

Whole Group/Independent

Have children re-sort their cards. Then read *The Ship* with children. Have them listen for and raise their hand when they hear words that begin with the sounds of *ch* and *sh*.

Have children find picture cards to match words in the text. *(ship, shoe, shell)* Then have them find another word in the story that begins with *sh*. *(shark)*

Day 4

Apply the Skill

Independent/Partner

Have children sort their cards again. Then have children turn to page 50 in their Word Study Notebook. Read aloud the directions. Have children work independently or with a partner to draw pictures of things that begin with *ch* and *sh* and then write those letters on the lines provided.

Day 5

Complete the Sort

Whole Group/Independent

Paste in Place

Have children turn to page 49 in their Word Study Notebook. Encourage children to sort their pictures according to their beginning sound. Then have them paste the pictures in the correct column for each beginning sound.

Play the Game

When children are finished, they may play the Bingo! game. (See the Teacher Resource CD for the game board, playing cards, and directions.)

Building Vocabulary

Even if children identify a chimney, they may not understand its purpose. Help children understand that a chimney is needed to carry away smoke from a fireplace or furnace below. Discuss why homes in the past had larger or more chimneys than many homes today.

ESL/ELL English Language Learners

Help children strengthen concepts while practicing pronunciation and usage. Begin by displaying the picture cards, choosing two at a time, and showing each at the place you use them in a sentence. Examples: "I am wearing a *shoe* and a *shirt*. Are you?" and "I have a *chair* and a *shelf* in my home. Do you?" Have children form sentences using the target words to answer the questions.

Challenge Words Activity

List the challenge words on the board or on chart paper. Guide children's reading of the list. Then ask volunteers to use the words in sentences.

Teacher Tip

Previously learned word families can be used to demonstrate that the sound of *ch* is different from the sound of either *c* or *h* and the sound of *sh* is different from the sound of *s* or *h*. Write and have children read these words with you: *cat, hat, chat; sip, hip, ship*. Tell children that they should look at all the letters of written words.

Sort 13

Consonant Digraphs th, wh

Objectives

- To identify the digraphs *th* and *wh*
- To identify and sort pictures with *th* and *wh*

Materials

Big Book of Rhymes, Level A, "What Do You Think?," page 25

Teacher Resource CD, Level A

Word Study Notebook, Level A, pages 51–54

Words Their Way Library, Level A, *Who Has Whiskers?*

Teacher Resource CD, Level A, Concentration game

Pictures

th	*wh*
thirteen	white
think	whisker
thick	whale
thorn	wheelbarrow
thimble	whistle
thumb	wheat

Challenge Words

that	whip
thud	when

Day 1 — Introduce the Sort

Whole Group

Read a Rhyme: "What Do You Think?"

Introduce words with the target sounds by reading the poem, "What Do You Think?" Reread the first sentence and have children find the word *think*. Write *think* on the board and underline the *th*. Tell children that the beginning sound of *think* is spelled with two letters. Repeat the routine with the word *whale*. Read the poem again, omitting some of the target words, and have children supply them.

Introduce Picture Sort th, wh

If you have not already done so, print and cut apart the picture cards for Sort 13 from the Teacher Resource CD. Introduce the pictures and define in context picture names that may be unfamiliar to children, such as *thick, thimble, wheelbarrow, whisker,* and *wheat*. Then demonstrate for children how to sort the picture names by their beginning sound. Have children describe how the names for the pictures in each column are alike and which letters make each sound.

Day 2 — Practice the Sort

Whole Group/Independent/Partner

You may want to begin Days 2–5 by rereading the rhyme from Day 1. Then review the previous day's sort demonstration. Help children tear out page 51 from their Word Study Notebook and cut apart the cards.

Have children work independently or with a partner to say the name of each picture and, using the grid on page 53 of their Word Study Notebook, sort the cards by their beginning sound.

Alternative Sort: What Is Alike?

When children are comfortable with this week's sort, lead them to re-sort all pictures except the one depicting *think* into three columns of categories: things that grow (*thorn, thumb, whisker, whale, wheat*), things that cannot grow (*thimble, wheelbarrow*), and words that describe things (*thirteen, thick, white*).

Day 3
Find Words in Context

Whole Group/Independent/Partner

Have children re-sort their cards. Then read *Who Has Whiskers?* with children. Have them listen for any words that begin with the sounds of *th* or *wh*.

Have children look through their picture cards to find the pictures for words in the text. *(whisker[s], white, whale)*

Day 4
Apply the Skill

Independent/Partner

Have children sort their cards again. Then have children turn to page 54 in their Word Study Notebook. Read aloud the directions. Have children work independently or with a partner to draw pictures of things that begin with *th* or *wh* and then write those letters on the lines provided.

Day 5
Complete the Sort

Whole Group/Independent

Paste in Place

Have children turn to page 53 in their Word Study Notebook. Encourage children to sort their pictures and words according to the beginning sound of each picture name. Then have them paste the pictures in the correct column for each beginning sound and letters.

Play the Game

When children are finished, they may play the Concentration game. (See the Teacher Resource CD for the playing cards and directions.)

Building Vocabulary

Clarify the meaning of *thick*. Ask children how they or someone else have used *thick* to tell about things. Children can then take turns asking and answering such questions as "Would you like to have a thick sandwich or a thin sandwich?"

ESL/ELL English Language Learners

Lead children in focusing on how the two different sounds of the digraphs are made. Have children hold a hand in front of their mouth and say *wh-wh-whale* and *th-th-think*. Have them repeat the routine with the words *white* and *thumb*. Point out the placement of the tongue when forming the two different sounds.

Challenge Words Activity

List the Challenge Words on the board or on chart paper, and encourage children to pronounce each word. Then invite volunteers to use the words in sentences.

Teacher Tip

If children note that *th* has a different sound in words such as *then, that, this,* and *the,* it is an opportunity to begin comparative lists and compliment children on good thinking about words.

Consonant Digraphs sh, ch, wh, th

Objectives

- To identify and review consonant digraphs
- To identify and sort pictures with *sh, ch, wh,* or *th*

Materials

 Big Book of Rhymes, Level A, "Watch Out, Sheep!," page 27

 Teacher Resource CD, Level A

 Word Study Notebook, Level A, pages 55–58

 Words Their Way Library, Level A, *Three White Sheep*

 Teacher Resource CD, Level A, Shear the Sheep game

Pictures		
sh	*ch*	*wh*
shoe	chin	wheelbarrow
ship	chick	wheel
shirt	chain	whistle
shelf	chair	whisker
shell	cheese	whale
th		
thirteen		
thick		
thimble		
thermometer		
thorn		

Day 1 Introduce the Sort

Whole Group

 Read a Rhyme: "Watch Out, Sheep!"

Introduce words with the target sounds by reading the poem "Watch Out, Sheep!" Reread the poem, and encourage children to listen for words beginning with *sh, ch, wh,* or *th. (sheep, chugs, when, thump)* Write each word on the chalkboard, and underline the beginning digraph. Remind children that two letters stand for one beginning sound in each word. Read the poem again, omitting the target words, and have children say them.

 Introduce Picture Sort *sh, ch, wh, th*

If you have not already done so, print and cut apart the picture cards for Sort 14 from the Teacher Resource CD. Introduce the pictures and define in context picture names that may be unfamiliar to children, such as *chick, chain, thimble,* and *whistle.* Then demonstrate for children how to sort the pictures by their beginning sounds. Have children describe how the picture names in each column are alike and which letters stand for each beginning sound.

Day 2 Practice the Sort

Whole Group/Independent/Partner

 You may want to begin Days 2–5 by rereading the rhyme from Day 1. Then review the previous day's sort demonstration. Help children tear out page 55 from their Word Study Notebook and cut apart the cards. Have children work independently or with a partner to say each picture name and, using the grid on page 57 of their Word Study Notebook, sort it by its beginning sound.

Alternative Sort: What Is Alike?

Display twelve pictures at a time, and have children take turns finding two or three pictures that show things that are alike in some way without telling how they are alike. As an example, *shoe* and *shirt* are things to wear; *chin* and *whisker* are found on a face. Invite volunteers to guess the category. When children can no longer pair pictures, replace some of them so new connections can be made.

Day 3
Find Words in Context

Whole Group/Independent

Have children re-sort their cards. Then read *Three White Sheep* with children. Have them listen for and identify any words that begin with the sounds of *ch*, *sh*, *wh*, and *th*.

Together, reread each spread of facing pages and have children point to the word that answers questions such as "Which word begins like *ship?*" (pages 2–3) Which word begins like *whistle?* (pages 4–5)."

Day 4
Apply the Skill

Independent/Partner

Have children sort their cards again. Then have children turn to page 58 in their Word Study Notebook. Read aloud the directions. Have children work independently or with a partner to draw pictures of things that begin with *sh*, *ch*, *wh*, or *th* and then write those letters on the lines provided.

Day 5
Complete the Sort

Whole Group/Independent

Paste in Place

Have children turn to page 57 in their Word Study Notebook. Encourage children to say the name of each picture and sort the cards by their beginning sound. Then have them paste the pictures into the correct column for each beginning sound.

Play the Game

When children are finished, they may play the Shear the Sheep game. (See the Teacher Resource CD for the game board, playing cards, and directions.)

Building Vocabulary

Use *whistle* in a sentence as a noun, but explain that *whistle* can be an object, action, or sound. Model for the class how to use *whistle* in a sentence with the other meanings. Then invite children to use *whistle* in sentences and tell what it means in each.

ESL/ELL English Language Learners

Children may need key mnemonic devices to remember the four digraph sounds and spellings. Discuss and draw outlines of a whale, a shirt, a chain, and a thorn with labels such as *whale*, and post the sound/letter devices in the classroom for reference. Children can draw pictures and write the words in the outlines.

Teacher Tip

Extend practice of the skill by having children go on a hunt for more examples of *sh*, *ch*, *wh*, and *th* pictures and words in books and magazines. Make time for sharing the results.

Beginning Consonants and Blends s, t, st

Objectives

- To identify the sounds of consonants *s*, *t*, and the *st* blend
- To identify, differentiate, and sort pictures with *s*, *t*, and *st*

Materials

 Big Book of Rhymes, Level A, "Stan Is Sad," page 29

 Teacher Resource CD, Level A

 Word Study Notebook, Level A, pages 59–62

 Words Their Way Library, Level A, *My Lost Top*

 Teacher Resource CD, Level A, Match! game

Pictures

s	t	st
sun	tag	steak
soap	tire	stamp
saw	tiger	steps
sit	tape	star
seal	top	stove

Challenge Words

set	tab	stun
sob		stack
		stub

Day 1 — Introduce the Sort

Whole Group

 Read a Rhyme: "Stan Is Sad"

Introduce words with the target sounds by reading the poem "Stan Is Sad." As you read, emphasize words that begin with *s*, *t*, or *st*. Read the poem again, and ask children to listen for and raise their hand when they hear words that begin with *s*, *t*, or *st*. Lead children in saying "*St-St-Stan, s-s-sad, t-t-top*" to compare the beginning sounds. Read the poem again, omitting the target words, and have children supply the missing words.

 Introduce Picture Sort *s*, *t*, *st*

Print and cut apart the picture cards for Sort 15 from the Teacher Resource CD. Introduce the pictures and define in context picture names that may be unfamiliar to children, such as *steak*, *stove*, and *seal*. Then demonstrate for children how to say the picture names and sort them by their beginning sound. Have children describe how the picture names in each column are alike and which letter or letters stand for each beginning sound.

Day 2 — Practice the Sort

Whole Group/Independent/Partner

 You may want to begin Days 2–5 by rereading the rhyme from Day 1. Then review the previous day's sort demonstration. Help children tear out page 59 from their Word Study Notebook and cut apart the picture cards.

Have children work independently or with a partner to say each picture name and, using the grid on page 61 of their Word Study Notebook, sort the cards by their beginning sound.

> **Alternative Sort: Odd One Out**
>
> Lead children to make connections between items pictured. Display all the pictures, and pull sets of three pictures at a time in which two items can be categorized as the same but one is very different. Demonstration sets: <u>sun</u>, <u>star</u>, tag (things in the sky); tire, <u>steak</u>, <u>stove</u> (things in a kitchen). Have children explain how two are alike and why the third does not belong. Let children take over the building of sets as the activity continues.

Day 3 — Find Words in Context

Whole Group/Independent/Partner

Have children re-sort their cards. Then read *My Lost Top* with children. Have them listen for and identify any words that begin with the sound of *s, t,* or *st.*

Together, reread each spread of facing pages and have children point to the word that answers questions such as "Which word begins like *tiger?*" (pages 2–3); "Which word begins like *stamp?*" (pages 6–7); Which word begins like *sun?* (pages 10–11)." Children can reread the book independently or with a partner.

Day 4 — Apply the Skill

Independent/Partner

Have children sort their cards again. Then have children turn to page 62 in their Word Study Notebook. Read aloud the directions. Have children work independently or with a partner to draw pictures of things that begin with *s, t,* or *st,* and then write those letters on the lines provided.

Day 5 — Complete the Sort

Whole Group/Independent

Paste in Place

Have children turn to page 61 in their Word Study Notebook. Encourage children to say the name of each picture and sort their cards according to beginning sound. Then have them paste the pictures in the correct column for the beginning sound and letters.

Play the Game

When children are finished, they may play the Match! game. (See the Teacher Resource CD for the playing cards and directions.)

Building Vocabulary

Show the stove picture, and emphasize that *stove* is one word for the object. Ask children to share other words they have heard or used to name the item in the picture. Invite children to tell about other kinds of stoves they've seen.

ESL/ELL English Language Learners

Focus on meaning and speedy recall of the pictures and words for *st.* You may need to discuss that a *steak* is one kind of meat, *steps* also can be called *stairs* (which also begins with *st*), and that a *stove* is like an oven.

Challenge Words Activity

Write each Challenge Word on a card. Show each card and invite volunteers to say the word. Then have children sort the cards into words that begin with *s, t,* or *st.*

Teacher Tip

Extend skill practice in this and following lessons by beginning a set of ongoing consonant-blend classroom books. This week, provide blank pages fastened together, either cut in the shape of a star or with a large star drawn on the cover. Have children add drawings, pictures, and words from magazines that begin like *star.*

Sort 16

Consonant Blends sp, sk, sm

Objectives

- To identify *s* blends
- To identify, differentiate, and sort pictures by *sp, sk,* or *sm* blends

Materials

 Big Book of Rhymes, Level A, "My Special Skill," page 31

 Teacher Resource CD, Level A

 Word Study Notebook, Level A, pages 63–66

 Words Their Way Library, Level A, *A Fun Place to Eat*

 Teacher Resource CD, Level A, Let's Skateboard game

Pictures

sp	sk	sm
spill	skis	smoke
spider	skate	smock
spear	skunk	smell
sponge	sky	smile
splash	skirt	

Challenge Words

spin	skin	smack
spun	skill	
	skull	

Day 1 — Introduce the Sort

Whole Group

Read a Rhyme: "My Special Skill"

Introduce words with the target sounds by reading the poem "My Special Skill." As you read, emphasize words that begin with *sp, sk,* or *sm.* Reread the poem and ask children to listen for words in the poem that begin with *sp, sk,* or *sm.* List the words in columns on the chalkboard or on chart paper, and point out to children that the words in each column begin with the same sound. Read the poem again, omitting the target words, and have children provide them.

Introduce Picture Sort *sp, sk, sm*

If you have not already done so, print and cut apart the picture cards for Sort 16 from the Teacher Resource CD. Introduce the pictures and words, and define in context picture names that may be unfamiliar to children, such as *spear, skis,* and *smock.* Then demonstrate for children how to sort the pictures by the beginning sound. Have children describe how the names of the pictures in each column are alike and which letters stand for each beginning sound.

Day 2 — Practice the Sort

Whole Group/Independent/Partner

 You may want to begin Days 2–5 by rereading the rhyme from Day 1. Then review the previous day's sort demonstration. Help children tear out page 63 from their Word Study Notebook and cut apart the picture cards. Have children work independently or with a partner to say the name of each picture and, using the grid on page 65 of their Word Study Notebook, sort the cards by their beginning blend.

Alternative Sort: Odd One Out

Display all the pictures and pull sets of three pictures at a time in which two items can be categorized the same but one is very different. Demonstration sets: *skis, skate, spider* (things people put on their feet, or things used in sports); *sponge, smock, skirt* (clothing). Have children explain how the two pictures are alike and why the third does not belong. Allow children to take over the building of sets as the activity continues.

Day 3 Find Words in Context

Whole Group/Independent/Partner

Have children re-sort their cards. Then read *A Fun Place to Eat* with children. Have them listen for and identify any words that begin with the sound of *sp*. Together, reread pages 4–5 and then pages 6–7, having children point to the word that answers the question "Which word begins like *spill?*" *(spin and spoon)* Children can next reread the book independently or with a partner. (They will also be practicing the previously learned *st* blend in the words *still* and *stamp.*)

Day 4 Apply the Skill

Independent/Partner

Have children sort their cards again. Then have children turn to page 66 in their Word Study Notebook. Read aloud the directions. Have children work independently or with a partner to draw pictures of things that begin with *sp, sk,* or *sm,* and then write those letters on the lines provided.

Day 5 Complete the Sort

Whole Group/Independent

Paste in Place

Have children turn to page 65 in their Word Study Notebook. Encourage them to say the name of each picture and sort the cards according to their beginning sound. Then have them paste the pictures in the correct column for the beginning sound and letters.

Play the Game

When children are finished, they may play the Let's Skateboard game. (See the Teacher Resource CD for the game board, playing cards, and directions.)

Building Vocabulary

Children may not recognize a smock or recall its name. Discuss how the picture shows clues about the smock and its use. Clarify that a smock is a loose outer shirt worn to protect clothing, and then have children suggest times a smock could be used.

ESL/ELL English Language Learners

If children are confusing the *s* blends when they speak, use the picture cards to focus on one blend each day. After several blends have been reviewed, show all the picture cards, and have children repeat the picture names after you. Shuffle the cards, and then have children take turns saying the picture names.

Challenge Words Activity

List the Challenge Words on the board or on chart paper. With children, decode each word. Then ask volunteers to use the words in sentences.

Teacher Tip

If children notice that some words beginning with *sc* have the same blended sounds as *sk* words, compliment them on their discovery and help them begin a comparative list. The list can be used and added to in the following lesson.

Consonant Blends sc, sn, sw

Objectives

- To identify the sounds of consonant blends with *s*
- To identify, differentiate, and sort pictures by *sc, sn,* and *sw* blends

Materials

Big Book of Rhymes, Level A, "I Fly So High," page 33

Teacher Resource CD, Level A

Word Study Notebook, Level A, pages 67–70

Words Their Way Library, Level A, *Sally's Spaceship*

Teacher Resource CD, Level A, Swinging High game

Pictures

sc	sn	sw
scale	snake	sweater
scooter	snow	swan
scout	snowman	switch
scarf	snail	swing
school	snap	swim

Challenge Words

scat	snap	swig
scam	snip	
	snug	

Day 1 Introduce the Sort

Whole Group

Read a Rhyme: "I Fly So High"

Introduce words with the target sounds by reading the poem "I Fly So High." Read the poem several times, and have children listen for the words *swing, snag,* and *scare.* Have children raise their hand when they hear the words. Call attention to the sounds of *sc, sn,* and *sw.* Read the poem again, omitting the target words and have children say them.

Introduce Picture Sort sc, sn, sw

If you have not already done so, print and cut apart the picture cards for Sort 17 from the Teacher Resource CD. Introduce the pictures and words, and define in context picture names that may be unfamiliar to children, such as *scooter, scout, sneakers, snap,* and *switch.* Then demonstrate for children how to sort the picture names by their beginning sound.

Day 2 Practice the Sort

Whole Group/Independent/Partner

You may want to begin Days 2–5 by rereading the rhyme from Day 1. Then review the previous day's sort demonstration. Help children tear out page 67 from their Word Study Notebook and cut apart the picture cards.

Have children work independently or with a partner to say the name of each picture and, using the grid on page 69, sort the cards by their beginning blend.

> **Alternative Sort: What Is Alike?**
>
> When children are comfortable with this week's sort, lead them to make connections among the items pictured. Display ten pictures at a time, and have children take turns finding two or three pictures that show things that are alike in some way without revealing to the class how they are alike. Classmates can guess the similarity.

Day 3

Find Words in Context

Whole Group/Independent/Partner

Have children re-sort their cards. Then read *Sally's Spaceship* with children. Have children listen for and identify words that begin with the sounds of *sn*. Reread together pages 6–7, having children point to the word that begins like *snow (snack)*. Have children locate words beginning with the previously learned *sp* and *st* blends in the words *spaceship* and *stars*.

Children can reread the book independently or with a partner.

Day 4

Apply the Skill

Independent/Partner

Have children sort their cards again. Then have children turn to page 70 in their Word Study Notebook. Read aloud the directions. Have children work independently or with a partner to draw pictures of things whose names begin with the *sc*, *sn*, or *sw* blend and then write the letters *sc*, *sn*, or *sw* under each picture.

Day 5

Complete the Sort

Whole Group/Independent/Partners

Paste in Place

Have children turn to page 69 in their Word Study Notebook. Encourage them to say the name of each picture and sort their cards according to their beginning sound. Then have them paste the picture cards in place on the page.

Play the Game

When children are finished, they may play the Swinging High game (See the Teacher Resource CD for the game board, playing cards, and directions.)

Building Vocabulary

If children are not familiar with the word *scout*, explain that the girl shown in the photograph is a member of the Girl Scout organization and that is why she's wearing a uniform. Invite children who are members of the Girl Scouts or Boy Scouts to talk about some of the activities they participate in.

ESL/ELL English Language Learners

If children are confusing names of any pictures, having problems with pronunciation, or using incorrect *s* blends when they speak, hold up a picture card whose name begins with one of the blends. First emphasize the blend, drawing out the beginning sound: *sn, sn-sn-snail*. Then take turns with children forming sentences about a snail.

Challenge Words Activity

In random order, write the Challenge Words for this sort on the board or on chart paper and then write the labels *sc*, *sn*, and *sw*. Encourage volunteers to say the words and then copy them under the correct label.

Teacher Tip

During repeated sorts, do not correct children when they place a picture in the wrong column. When children have completed the sort, have them read the picture names aloud. If they still do not find the misplaced picture, tell children which column it is in, and have them find and correct the mistake.

Consonant Blends pl, sl, bl, fl

Objectives

- To identify the sounds of *l* blends
- To identify, differentiate, and sort pictures by *pl*, *sl*, *bl*, and *fl* blends

Materials

 Big Book of Rhymes, Level A, "Hurry to My Place!," page 35

 Teacher Resource CD, Level A

 Word Study Notebook, Level A, pages 71–74

 Words Their Way Library, Level A, *Glenda the Lion*

 Teacher Resource CD, Level A, Pool Play game

Pictures

pl	sl	bl	fl
plant	sled	blocks	flag
plow	sliced	black	flowers
plug	sleep	blue	flute
pliers	slippers	blanket	float
playpen	slide	blouse	flashlight

Challenge Words

plan	slip	blot	flip
plum	slug	bland	flap

Day 1

Introduce the Sort

Whole Group

 Read a Rhyme: "Hurry to My Place!"

Introduce the target sounds by reading the poem "Hurry to My Place!" Read the poem several times to have children listen for words that begin *pl, sl, bl,* or *fl*. As you emphasize the target words, invite children to join in the readings.

 Introduce Picture Sort *pl, sl, bl, fl*

If you have not already done so, print and cut apart the picture cards for Sort 18 from the Teacher Resource CD. Introduce the pictures and words, and define in context picture names that may be unfamiliar to children, such as *plow, pliers, sliced, blindfold, float,* and *flute*. Then demonstrate for children how to sort the pictures by the beginning sound of the picture name. Have children describe how the picture names in each column are alike and which letter stands for each sound.

Day 2

Practice the Sort

Whole Group/Independent/Partner

You may want to begin Days 2–5 by rereading the rhyme from Day 1. Then review the previous day's sort demonstration. Help children tear out page 71 from their Word Study Notebook and cut apart the cards.

Have children work independently or with a partner to say the name of each picture and, using the grid on page 73 in their Word Study Notebook, sort the picture cards by beginning sound.

> **Alternative Sort: Odd One Out**
> Display all the pictures and pull sets of three pictures at a time in which two items can be categorized the same but one is very different. Demonstration sets: *plant, flowers, blanket* (things in a garden); *flashlight, blocks, playpen* (things for a baby). Have children explain how two are alike and why the third does not belong. Allow children to take over the building of sets as the activity continues.

Find Words in Context

Whole Group/Independent/Partner

Have children re-sort their cards. Then read *Glenda the Lion* with children. Have them first listen for any words that begin with the *l* sound. Then have them listen for words that begin with an *l* blend that they have been sorting this week. Help children find and point to the words *black, play, sleeping,* and *slow*. Encourage children to reread the book independently or with a partner.

Apply the Skill

Independent/Partner

Have children sort their cards again. Then have children turn to page 74 in their Word Study Notebook. Read aloud the directions. Then have children work independently or with a partner to draw pictures of things whose names begin with *pl, sl, bl,* or *fl,* and then write each blend under the corresponding pictures.

Complete the Sort

Whole Group/Independent

Paste in Place

Have children turn to page 73 in their Word Study Notebook. Encourage them to say the name of each picture and then sort the cards according to their beginning sound. Then have them paste the pictures in place on the page.

Play the Game

When children are finished, they may play the Pool Play game. (See the Teacher Resource CD for the game board, playing cards, and directions.)

Building Vocabulary

Help children understand more about a plow. Ask children to describe two kinds of plows. If necessary, explain that there are farm plows and snowplows. Help children summarize that a plow uses large blades to push or turn over and move soil or snow.

ESL/ELL English Language Learners

Help children better understand English usage and what some of the pictured items are by making comparisons. If possible, make simple sketches of other items for comparison, as necessary. The following can be discussed: a *playpen* is not a crib; a *plow* is only one kind of farm or gardening equipment; a *plug* is not the same thing as a cord; *pliers* are one kind of many tools; something *sliced* usually means cut by a knife; a *blouse* is not a boy's shirt; a *flute* is not the same thing as a horn.

Challenge Words Activity

Write each Challenge Word on a card, and make copies of the words to distribute to children. As they work in small groups, encourage children to say the words and sort them according to their beginning blend. Then ask volunteers to say sentences using the words.

Teacher Tip

For quick and frequent skill practice or informal assessment, have children hold up *pl, sl, bl,* or *fl* cards that show the beginning sound in words you call.

Consonant Blends cr, cl, fr, gl, gr

Objectives

- To identify the sounds of *r* and *l* blends
- To identify, differentiate, and sort pictures by *cr*, *cl*, *fr*, *gl*, and *gr* blends

Materials

 Big Book of Rhymes, Level A, "The River Frog," page 37

 Teacher Resource CD, Level A

 Word Study Notebook, Level A, pages 75–78

 Words Their Way Library, Level A, *The River Grows*

 Teacher Resource CD, Level A, Match! Game

Pictures

cr	cl	fr	gl	gr
crane	cloud	fry	glue	grass
crown	claw	fruit	glasses	grill
crib	clock	frame	glass	grasshopper
crackers	class	freezer	globe	groceries

Challenge Words

crop	clan	frill	glad	grip
	clap	fret		
	clip			

Introduce the Sort

Whole Group

Read a Rhyme: "The River Frog"

Read "The River Frog" to children. Write the word *frog* on the board and underline *fr*. Say the word *frog* emphasizing the initial *fr*. Remind children that *fr* is a consonant blend—two sounds that blend together but each sound is still heard. Reread the poem and ask children to raise their hand when they hear words in the poem that begin with the consonant blend *cr*, *cl*, *fr*, *gl*, or *gr*. (*croaks, clamps, frog, green, gray*)

Introduce Picture Sort *cr, cl, fr, gl, gr*

Print and cut apart the picture cards for Sort 19 from the Teacher Resource CD. Introduce the pictures and words, and define in context picture names that may be unfamiliar to children, such as *fry, crane, claw,* and *globe*. Show children how to sort the picture names according to their beginning consonant blend. Have volunteers name the pictures in the columns and identify the consonant blend common to each word.

Practice the Sort

Whole Group/Independent/Partner

You may want to begin Days 2–5 by rereading the rhyme from Day 1. Then review the previous day's card sort demonstration. Help children tear out page 75 from their Word Study Notebook and cut apart the cards.

Have children work independently or with a partner to say the name of each picture and, using the grid on page 77 in their Word Study Notebook, sort the cards by their beginning consonant blend.

Alternative Sort: Inside or Outside

When children have completed this week's sort, set aside the card for *fry* and hold up the remaining cards, one by one. Ask children if the item on the card would *usually* be found outside or inside. Sort the cards into an "outside" pile and an "inside" pile. You may wish to also include an "inside and outside" category.

Day 3

Find Words in Context

Whole Group

Have children re-sort their cards. Then read *The River Grows* to children. Then give each child a picture card. Explain that you will read the story again as each child listens for the blend on his or her cards. A blend may be used many times, once, or not at all. When a child hears a blend, he or she should hold up the picture card. During the reading allow the child to point out the place in the story where the blend is used.

Day 4

Apply the Skill

Independent/Partner

Have children sort their cards again. Then have children turn to page 78 in their Word Study Notebook. Read the directions aloud. Let children work independently or with a partner to draw pictures of other items that begin with *cr, cl, fr, gl,* or *gr.* Have them write the corresponding beginning sound below each picture.

Day 5

Complete the Sort

Whole Group/Independent

Paste in Place

Have children turn to page 77 in their Word Study Notebook. Encourage them to say the name of each picture and sort their cards according to their beginning blend (*cr, cl, fr, gl, gr*). Then have children paste the pictures in place on the page.

Play the Game

When children have finished, allow time for them to play the Match! game. (See the Teacher Resource CD for playing cards and directions.)

Building Vocabulary

If children confuse claws, toes, and feet, explain that claws are sharp, hooked nails on a bird's or an animal's feet. Ask children to name animals that have claws. Nonfiction books or magazines can be used to find pictures for comparing claws.

ESL/ELL English Language Learners

Review the cards with children, naming each picture. Explain to children that sometimes a word may be used to label two different things. For example, the word *glasses* might refer to either drinking containers or eyewear. Similarly, the word *crane* might refer to a long-legged bird or to a machine with a long arm for moving objects.

Challenge Words Activity

Ask children to think of other words that begin with *cr, cl, fr, gl, gr.* If children need prompting, make suggestions from the Challenge Words list. Then have children make word cards for these new words, as well as the Challenge Words. Encourage children to work in pairs or small groups to sort the words according to their beginning blend.

Teacher Tip

When you introduce a new card, you can quickly check children's pronunciation and understanding by asking children to use the word in a sentence.

Sort 20

Consonant Blends pr, tr, dr, br

Objectives

- To identify the sounds of *r*-blends
- To identify, differentiate, and sort pictures by *pr*, *tr*, *dr*, and *br* blends

Materials

 Big Book of Rhymes, Level A, "Sack Race," page 39

 Teacher Resource CD, Level A

 Word Study Notebook, Level A, pages 79–82

 Words Their Way Library, Level A, *At the Track*

 Teacher Resource CD, Level A, Sack Race Game

Pictures

pr	tr	dr	br
princess	tray	dragon	bread
prize	track	draw	brush
prince	triangle	dream	bridge
pretzel	tree	drill	broom
present	truck	drum	bride

Challenge Words

prance	trap	drag	bran
proud	trip	drip	Brad
prime	trot	drop	brag
		drug	

Day 1 — Introduce the Sort

Whole Group

 ### Read a Rhyme: "Sack Race"

Read the poem "Sack Race" to children, emphasizing words beginning with the consonant blends *pr*, *tr*, *dr*, or *br*. Write *pr* on the chalkboard and tell children that /p/ and /r/ blend together to form the sound of this blend. Reread the poem, and ask children to raise their hand when they hear the word in the poem that begins with *pr*. (prizes) Pronounce the word together, emphasizing the beginning consonant blend. Continue in the same manner with *tr*, *dr*, and *br*. (track, dream, Bravo)

 ### Introduce Picture Sort *pr, tr, dr, br*

Print and cut apart the cards for Sort 20 from the Teacher Resource CD. Introduce the pictures and define in context picture names that may be unfamiliar to children, such as *prince*, *tray*, *drill*, and *bride*. Show children how to sort the picture names according to their beginning consonant blend. Have volunteers name the pictures in the columns and identify the beginning blend common to each word.

Day 2 — Practice the Sort

Whole Group/Independent/Partner

 You may want to begin Days 2–5 by rereading the rhyme from Day 1. Then review the previous day's sort demonstration. Help children remove page 79 from their Word Study Notebook and cut apart the picture cards. Have children work independently or with a partner to say the name of each picture and, using the grid on page 81, sort the cards by their beginning consonant blend.

Alternative Sort: What Is Alike?

Display twelve pictures at a time and have children take turns finding two or three pictures that show things alike in some way without telling how they are alike. As an example, *truck*, *tree*, and *bridge* are things seen on the road. Invite volunteers to guess the category. When children can no longer pair pictures, replace some of them so new connections can be made.

54

Day 3   Find Words in Context

Whole Group

Have children re-sort their cards. Then show children the cover of the book *At the Track*. Identify Brad and Fred on the cover. Point out the *r* blends at the beginning of the two names. Have children listen for other words in the book that begin with *r* blends. (*brag, drops, track, trips*)

Day 4   Apply the Skill

Independent/Partner

Have children sort their cards again. Then have children turn to page 82 in their Word Study Notebook. Read the directions aloud. Let children work independently or with partners to draw pictures of other items that begin with *pr*, *tr*, *dr*, or *br*. Children should draw two pictures for each consonant blend and write the blend below the corresponding picture.

Day 5   Complete the Sort

Whole Group/Independent

Paste in Place

Have children turn to page 81 in their Word Study Notebook. Encourage them to say the name of each picture and sort their cards by their beginning sound. Have children paste the pictures in place on the page.

Play the Game

When children have finished, let them play the Sack Race game. (See the Teacher Resource CD for game board, playing cards, and directions.)

Building Vocabulary

Children may recognize a basic triangle, but make sure they know that a triangle has three sides and points. Draw different shapes, including triangles of varying side lengths and angles, and have children say which shapes are triangles.

ESL/ELL English Language Learners

For practice making simple sentences and pronouncing words with *r* blends, pair an English language learner with a native speaker and ask them to select from picture cards to complete this sentence: "I saw a _____ at the _____." Encourage children to use different card combinations to create as many different sentences as possible.

Challenge Words Activity

List the Challenge Words on the board or on chart paper. With children, decode each word. Then ask volunteers to use the words in sentences.

Teacher Tip

To model blending, hold a *d* letter card in one hand and an *r* letter card in the other. Have children say the sounds for each letter. Then move the cards together and have children blend the sounds.

Beginning Sounds k, wh, qu, tw

Objectives

- To identify the beginning sounds of *k*, *wh*, *qu*, and *tw*
- To identify, differentiate, and sort pictures by beginning sounds *k*, *wh*, *qu*, and *tw*

Materials

 Big Book of Rhymes, Level A, "Whales Can Do Tricks," page 41

 Teacher Resource CD, Level A

 Word Study Notebook, Level A, pages 83–86

 Words Their Way Library, Level A, *Humpback Whales*

 Teacher Resource CD, Level A, Concentration Game

Pictures

k	wh	qu	tw
kangaroo	wheelbarrow	question	twenty
kitten	whistle	quack	twine
key	wheat	quilt	twig
kite	whisker	queen	twelve
kick	whale	quiet	twins

Challenge Words

kin	whip	quit	twin
	when		

Day 1 Introduce the Sort

Whole Group

 Read a Rhyme: "Whales Can Do Tricks"

Write *killer whale* on the board. Underline the beginning sounds *k* and *wh*, and pronounce the two words. Discuss killer whales, explaining that they use their sharp teeth to feed on fish and ocean animals. Read the poem "Whales Can Do Tricks," emphasizing words beginning with *k*, *wh*, *qu*, and *tw*. (*killer, quick, when, twirls, twist*) Reread the poem several times and ask children to raise their hand when they hear a word that begins with the sound *k*, *wh*, *qu*, or *tw*.

 Introduce Picture Sort k, wh, qu, tw

Print and cut apart the cards for Sort 21 from the Teacher Resource CD. Introduce the pictures and define in context picture names that may be unfamiliar to children, such as *quiet*, *twine*, and *twig*. Show children how to say the picture names and then sort them according to their beginning sound. Have volunteers name the pictures in the columns and identify the beginning sound common to each word.

Day 2 Practice the Sort

Whole Group/Independent/Partner

 You may want to begin Days 2–5 by rereading the rhyme from Day 1. Then review the previous day's sort demonstration. Help children to remove page 83 from their Word Study Notebook and cut apart the picture cards. Have children work independently or with a partner to say the name of each picture and, using the grid on page 85 of their Word Study Notebook, sort the cards by their beginning sound.

Alternative Sort: I Spy

Set up the classroom in advance so that there are many objects from the cards within view. For example, place some keys and a ball of twine on your desk, and write a question and the numbers 12 and 20 on the board. Have children sort their cards into two piles, one pile for the things they can see from their desks (either in the classroom or out the window) and one pile for things they cannot see.

Day 3

Find Words in Context

Whole Group

Have children re-sort their cards. Then turn to the last page of the book *Humpback Whales*. Ask children what kind of whale is shown in the diagram. Let volunteers describe the humpback whale and name its body parts. Say the word *whale*, and ask children to identify the beginning sound. (/wh/) Then have children listen for *wh* words as you read the book. Write the words on the board. *(whale, what, where)* Compare the sound of *wh* to the sound of *w*. (Words in the book that begin with *w* include *watch*, *way*, and *we*.)

Day 4

Apply the Skill

Independent/Partner

Have children sort their cards again. Then read aloud the directions on page 86 of the Word Study Notebook. Have children work independently or with partners to draw pictures of other items that begin with *k, wh, qu,* or *tw*. Have children write the corresponding beginning sound below each picture.

Day 5

Complete the Sort

Whole Group/Independent

Paste in Place

Have children turn to page 85 in their Word Study Notebook. Encourage them to say the name of each picture and sort their cards according to their beginning sound. Have children paste the pictures in place on the page.

Play the Game

When children have finished, let them play the Concentration game. (See the Teacher Resource CD for the playing cards and directions.)

Building Vocabulary

Help children understand the meaning of the word *question* by explaining that it is a sentence that asks for something. Display the picture card and tell them that it shows a question mark—a kind of punctuation that is always found at the end of a question.

ESL/ELL English Language Learners

Bring actual items into the classroom to help explain words that may be unfamiliar to children. If possible, include a ball of twine and a quilt. Identify the items and have children repeat their names and use each word in a sentence.

Challenge Words Activity

Help children brainstorm other words that begin with *k, wh, qu,* and *tw*. Refer to the Challenge Word list, as necessary. Then have children make word cards for these new words, as well as the Challenge Words. Encourage them to work in pairs or small groups to sort the words into categories.

Teacher Tip

You can add variety to the sorting activities by letting children sort picture cards into different types of containers. Try using boxes, lunch bags, grocery bags, baskets, or plastic containers. Tape or clip a label onto each container.

 Spell Check 3

After completing Sorts 12–21, you may want to administer Spell Check 3 in the Word Study Notebook on page 157. See page 19 for instructions on assessment.

Word Families -at, -ot, -it

Objectives

- To recognize and read words in word families -at,- ot, and -it
- To identify and sort pictures and words with -at,- ot, and -it

Materials

 Big Book of Rhymes, Level A, "The Cat," page 43

 Teacher Resource CD, Level A

 Word Study Notebook, Level A, pages 87–90

 Words Their Way Library, Level A, *Too High!*

Teacher Resource CD, Level A, Word Maker Game

Words			Pictures		
-at	-ot	-it	-at	-ot	-it
rat	not	fit	hat	pot	hit
sat	lot	bit	bat	cot	pit
fat	rot	quit	mat	dot	sit

Challenge Words

-at	-ot	-it
brat	plot	grit
flat	shot	skit
scat	trot	slit

Day 1 Introduce the Sort

Whole Group

Read a Rhyme: "The Cat"

Read the poem "The Cat" to children. After listening to the poem several times, have them listen for the last word in each line. *(cat, sat; hot, not; fit, sit)* Ask children if all the words rhyme (no), and why or why not (Ending sounds vary, and they are not all in the same word family.) Have children identify the pairs that do rhyme. Write the pairs on the board, *(cat sat; hot not; fit sit).*

Introduce Picture/Word Sort -at, -ot, -it

 Print and cut apart the picture/word cards for Sort 22 from the Teacher Resource CD. Introduce the words and pictures, and define in context words and picture names that may be unfamiliar to children, such as *rot* and *pit*. Show children how to sort the pictures and words into -at, -ot, and -it word families. Ask children how the words in each column are alike. *(They have the same endings, and are in the same word family.)*

Day 2 Practice the Sort

Whole Group/Partner/Independent

 You may want to begin Days 2–5 by rereading the rhyme from Day 1. Then review the previous day's sort demonstration. Help children remove page 87 from their Word Study Notebook and cut apart the cards.

Using the sorting grid on page 89, have children work independently or with partners to sort their cards into -at, -ot, and -it word families. Encourage children to say the names of the pictures and read the words as they work.

Alternative Sort: Places or Actions

After children have had success sorting the picture and word cards, invite them to sort the cards in a different way. Set aside cards for *fat*, *not*, and *lot*. Then have children sort the pictures and words for objects (*rat, hat, bat, mat, pot, cot, dot, pit*) and pictures and words for actions (*sat, rot, fit, bit, quit, hit, sit*). You may want to point out that some words, such as *fit*, *hit*, and *pit*, can have more than one meaning.

Day 3 Find Words in Context

Whole Group

Have children re-sort their cards. Then show children the cover of the book *Too High!* Ask children to look at the picture and explain what is too high. *(the balloon)* Ask children if they can find a word in the story that is in the same word family as *hot*. *(not)* Then ask if they can find a word in the same word family as *quit*. *(it)*

Day 4 Apply the Skill

Independent/Partner

Have children sort their cards again. Then read aloud the directions on page 90 of the Word Study Notebook. Guide children as they use the consonants at the top of the first column to think of and write words ending with -*at*. Then have children work independently or with partners to write words ending with -*ot* or -*it*.

Day 5 Complete the Sort

Whole Group/Independent

Paste in Place

Have children turn to page 89 in their Word Study Notebook. Ask them to say the name of each picture and word and sort their cards into -*at*, -*ot*, and -*it* word families. Have children paste their pictures and words into the correct columns on the page.

Play the Game

When children have finished, let them play the Word Maker game. (See the Teacher Resource CD for playing cards and directions.)

Building Vocabulary

Develop children's understanding of *rot*. Remind them that they have probably seen a rotten apple or banana, and ask how these fruits changed as they rotted. The group might experiment by leaving identical fruits in hot sunlight, in a darker location, and in water to observe which begins to rot first.

ESL/ELL English Language Learners

Review the words and pictures with children. Have children use the words to complete sentences such as "If I leave an apple core in the dirt, it will [rot]." or "The dog [bit] me because I teased it." Listen closely to be sure children are pronouncing the word endings correctly, and provide help as needed.

Challenge Words Activity

Give each child three blank word cards. Ask children to write a word on each card from the -*at*, -*ot*, or -*it* word families. If they need prompting, make suggestions from the Challenge Words. Collect the cards, shuffle them, and give one card to each child. Have children sort themselves into three groups, one for each word family. If needed, suggest places for the three groups to gather. There will be enough word cards to complete two additional whole-group sorts.

Teacher Tip

If two children are working together as partners to sort cards, remind them that both children should take part in the activity. Suggest that one child can place a card while the other child confirms the placement. Then children can switch roles.

You may wish to use the Sort 22 **Build, Blend, and Extend**. (See the Teacher Resource CD.)

Sort 23

Word Families -an, -un, -in

Objectives

- To recognize and read words in words families *-an*, *-un*, or *-in*
- To identify and sort pictures and words with *-an*, *-un*, or *-in*

Materials

 Big Book of Rhymes, Level A, "A Spin and a Grin," page 45

 Teacher Resource CD, Level A

 Word Study Notebook, Level A pages 91–94

 Words Their Way Library, Level A, *The Merry-Go-Round*

 Teacher Resource CD, Level A, In the Pocket Game

Words			Pictures		
-an	-un	-in	-an	-un	-in
plan	stun	tin	pan	bun	fin
tan	spun	grin	man	run	chin
ran	sun	win	fan	fun	twin

Challenge Words

-an	-un	-in
ban	pun	bin
clan	shun	shin
span		spin

Day 1 Introduce the Sort

Whole Group

 Read a Rhyme: "A Spin and a Grin"

After several readings of "A Spin and a Grin," write the last word of the first line *(grin)* and the last word of the second line *(spin)* on the board. Read the words, and ask children how they are the same. *(They rhyme.)* Let a volunteer underline the ending letters in each word *(in)*. Continue with the next two lines in the poem.

 Introduce Picture/Word Sort -an, -un, -in

Print and cut apart the picture/word cards for Sort 23 from the Teacher Resource CD. Introduce the words and pictures, and define in context words and picture names that may be unfamiliar to children, such as *stun, shun,* and *fun*. Show children how to sort the cards into *-an, -un,* and *-in* word families. Ask children how the words in each column are alike *(They have the same endings, and are in the same word family.)* Ask a volunteer to point out the column in which a word ending with *-an* belongs. Ask where words ending with *-un* or *-in* belong.

Day 2 Practice the Sort

Whole Group/Partner/Independent

  You may want to begin Days 2–5 by rereading the rhyme from Day 1. Then review the previous day's sort demonstration. Help children remove page 91 from their Word Study Notebook and cut apart the cards.

Have children work independently or with a partner to say the name of each picture or word and, using the grid on page 93, sort their cards into *-an, -un,* and *-in* word families.

Alternative Sort: Letter Count

When children have completed this week's sort, have them work independently or with partners to re-sort the word cards into piles according to the number of letters in each word. Children should make two piles, one for three-letter words and one for four-letter words.

Day 3 — Find Words in Context

Whole Group

Have children re-sort their cards. Then read *The Merry-Go-Round* to children. Then divide the class into three groups. Assign a different word family to each group *(-an, -un, -in)*. Reread the book and encourage each group to raise their hand when they hear words from their assigned word family. When you have finished reading the book, permit the groups to take turns telling which words they identified. *(ran, spun, run, spin, in)*

Day 4 — Apply the Skill

Independent/Partner

Have children sort their cards again. Then have children turn to page 94 of their Word Study Notebook. Read the directions aloud. Have children work independently or with partners to use the consonants provided to write on the lines words ending with *-an, -un,* or *-in.*

Day 5 — Complete the Sort

Whole Group/Independent

Paste in Place

Have children turn to page 93 in their Word Study Notebook. Ask children to say the name of each picture and word and then sort their cards into the three word families *(-an, -un,* and *-in)*. Have children paste the pictures in place on the page.

Play the Game

When children have finished, let them play the In the Pocket game. (See the Teacher Resource CD for playing cards and directions.)

Building Vocabulary

Explain that *stun* means "to shock in a great or a deep way." Give an example of news that would be stunning to you. Then have children tell what might stun someone and why. Encourage them to show how a stunned person might look.

ESL/ELL English Language Learners

Review the words and pictures with children. Have children pantomime, wherever possible, the picture and word meanings to be sure they understand their meanings.

Challenge Words Activity

Write *-an, -un,* and *-in* in large letters in columns on chart paper. Write either *-an, -un,* or *-in* on cards and provide one word card to each child. Explain that they should think of and write words that end with the word family listed on their card. If children need prompting, make suggestions from the Challenge Words list. Have children paste their card in the corresponding column.

Teacher Tip

If children become frustrated trying to brainstorm words in the same word family, suggest that they go through the alphabet, trying each consonant. Often this method quickly turns up many words. If you wish, permit children to occasionally experiment with made-up words, such as *gan* and *zan.*

You may wish to use the Sort 23 **Build, Blend, and Extend.** (See the Teacher Resource CD.)

Word Families -ad, -ed, -ab, -ob

Objectives

- To recognize and read short vowel words in four word families
- To identify and sort pictures and words ending with -ad, -ed, -ab, or -ob

Materials

 Big Book of Rhymes, Level A, "Bob's Sled," page 47

 Teacher Resource CD, Level A

 Word Study Notebook, Level A, pages 95–98

 Words Their Way Library, Level A, *Ted's Red Sled*

 Teacher Resource CD, Level A, Word Maker Game

Words				Pictures			
-ad	-ed	-ab	-ob	-ad	-ed	-ab	-ob
pad	fed	tab	rob	sad	wed	cab	cob
glad	led	grab	glob	mad	sled	crab	Bob
had	red	nab	mob				

Challenge Words

-ad	-ed	-ab	-ob
lad	bled	jab	gob
tad	shred	blab	snob
			knob

Day 1 — Introduce the Sort

Whole Group

 Read a Rhyme: "Bob's Sled"

Read the poem "Bob's Sled" to children and ask them to listen for words that rhyme. After reading, write the word endings -ad, -ed, -ab, and -ob on the chalkboard. Reread the first two lines of the poem, emphasizing the rhyming pair *glad* and *bad.* Ask children to identify the rhyming words, and write them below the corresponding label. Continue with the last four lines of the poem.

 Introduce Picture/Word Sort -ad, -ed, -ab, -ob

If you have not already done so, print and cut apart the picture/word cards for Sort 24 from the Teacher Resource CD. Introduce the words and pictures, and define in context words and picture names that may be unfamiliar to children, such as *tab, nab,* and *mob.* Then help children sort the pictures and words into word families. Ask children to describe how the words in each column are alike. *(They rhyme and have the same endings.)*

Day 2 — Practice the Sort

Whole Group/Independent/Partner

 You may want to begin Days 2–5 by rereading the rhyme from Day 1. Then review the previous day's sort demonstration. Help children tear out page 95 from their Word Study Notebook and cut apart the cards.

Have children work independently or with a partner to say the name of each picture and, using the grid on page 97 of their Word Study Notebook, sort the cards by their ending sound.

Alternative Sort: What I Feel

Discuss with children words that describe feelings. Following the discussion, have children work with a partner to sort the cards into words that name feelings and those that do not. Once the cards have been sorted, invite the first partner to pantomime one of the feeling words. After the other partner guesses the word, children can switch roles and repeat the activity.

Day 3 — Find Words in Context

Whole Group/Independent

Have children re-sort their cards. Then show children the cover of the book *Ted's Red Sled*. Ask a volunteer to read the title. Ask children which title words are in this week's sort. *(red, sled)* Lead children to recognize that all three words in the title rhyme because they are in the *-ed* word family. Read the book several times with children, pointing out the title words within the text. Challenge children to name the fourth word from the book that belongs to the *-ed* family. *(bed)* Have children look through their word cards to find words that match words in the text.

Day 4 — Apply the Skill

Independent/Partner

Have children sort their cards again. Then have children turn to page 98 in their Word Study Notebook. Read aloud the directions, and have children work independently or with a partner to use the given letters to write four words for each word family.

Day 5 — Complete the Sort

Whole Group/Independent

Paste in Place

Have children turn to page 97 in their Word Study Notebook. Encourage children to say the name of each picture and read each word. Then have them sort their cards according to *-ad, -ed, -ab,* and *-ob* word families. Then have children paste the cards in place on the page.

Play the Game

When children are finished, they may play the Word Maker game (See the Teacher Resource CD for the playing cards and directions.)

Building Vocabulary

Show a book or folder's tab, and tell how the tab helps you find something. Consider using a classroom book with sections or chapters to have children help you attach and label tabs in places that make sense.

ESL/ELL English Language Learners

After children have sorted their pictures and words into word families, pair them with a proficient speaker of English and invite them to use a tape recorder to record themselves reading the words and saying the picture names in each word family. Encourage children to replay the tape, listening to the pronunciations of the vowel sound in each word family.

Challenge Words Activity

Ask children to think of other words that end with *-ad, -ed, -ab,* or *-ob*. If children need prompting, make suggestions from the Challenge Words list. Then have children make word cards for these new words. Encourage children to work in pairs or small groups to sort the words into word families.

Teacher Tip

Listen as children complete the sorting activities. Check to be sure they are enunciating correctly in order to avoid mistakes in sorting.

You may wish to use the Sort 24 **Build, Blend, and Extend.** (See the Teacher Resource CD.)

Word Families -ag, -eg, -ig, -og, -ug

Objectives

- To recognize and read words in word families
- To identify and sort pictures and words ending with -ag, -eg, -ig, -og, or -ug

Materials

 Big Book of Rhymes, Level A, "Someday," page 49

 Teacher Resource CD, Level A

 Word Study Notebook, Level A, pages 99–102

 Words Their Way Library, Level A, *When We Are Big*

 Teacher Resource CD, Level A, Park Race Game

Words

-ag	-eg	-ig	-og	-ug
bag	Greg	big	bog	hug
sag	Meg	fig	fog	mug

Pictures

rag	beg	pig	log	bug
flag	peg	dig	dog	rug

Challenge Words

nag		gig	jog	tug
brag		rig	clog	chug

Day 1 Introduce the Sort

Whole Group

Read a Rhyme: "Someday"

Read the poem "Someday" aloud several times, emphasizing the rhyming words (*dogs, frogs, snug, hug*). Ask children to name the words that rhyme. Write the words in columns on the chalkboard or on chart paper. Ask children how the words in each column are alike. Reread the poem, omitting the target words, and have children provide them.

Introduce Picture/Word Sort -ag, -eg, -ig, -og, -ug

Print and cut apart the picture/word cards for Sort 25 from the Teacher Resource CD. Introduce the words and pictures, and define in context words and picture names that may be unfamiliar to children, such as *sag, bog,* and *fig.* Then demonstrate for children how to say the name of each picture and sort the picture cards into -ag, -eg, -ig, -og, and -ug word families. Ask children to tell how the words in each column are alike. (*They rhyme and have the same endings.*)

Day 2 Practice the Sort

Whole Group/Independent/Partner

You may want to begin Days 2–5 by rereading the rhyme from Day 1. Then review the previous day's sort demonstration. Help children remove page 99 from their Word Study Notebook and cut apart the word and picture cards.

Have children work independently or with a partner to say the name of each picture and word and, using the grid on page 101 of the Word Study Notebook, sort the cards into word families.

Alternative Sort: Animals, People, and More!

Ask children to sort the picture and word cards into three groups—animals, people, and things. After children complete the sort, have them tell who has two legs (*Greg, Meg*), what has more than two legs (*pig, dog, bug*), and what has no legs (*bog, fig, fog, bag, mug, rag, flag, peg, log, rug*).

Day 3 — Find Words in Context

Whole Group

Have children re-sort their cards. Then read aloud the book *When We Are Big*. Ask children to listen for the words *big, pig,* and *dog* and hold up the corresponding word or picture card when they hear it or see it in the story. Challenge children to identify an additional story word that belongs in the *-ig* word family. (*wig*)

Day 4 — Apply the Skill

Independent/Partner

Have children sort their cards again. Then have children turn to page 102 in their Word Study Notebook. Read aloud the directions, and have children work independently or with a partner to use the given letters to make three words for each word family.

Day 5 — Complete the Sort

Whole Group/Independent

Paste in Place

Have children turn to page 101 in their Word Study Notebook. Encourage children to say the name of each picture and word card and sort their cards into *-ag, -eg, -ig, -og,* and *-ug* word families. Then have them paste their cards in place on the page.

Play the Game

When children are finished, they may play the Park Race game (See the Teacher Resource CD for the game board, spinner, rhyming word sheet, and directions.)

Building Vocabulary

Explain if necessary that *sag* means "to bend or sink, especially in the middle," and make a sketch for the sentence: *These wooden shelves sag.* Call attention to using a final *s* as you also sketch for the sentence: *This rope sags.* Ask what other things can sag, and have children draw them.

ESL/ELL English Language Learners

It may be difficult for English Language Learners to hear and differentiate between the five short vowel sounds, thus making it difficult for them to complete the sort. To help them hear the vowel sound more easily, model how to slowly elongate the vowel sound when saying each word such as *baaaag*.

Challenge Words Activity

Help children brainstorm other words that end with *-ag, -eg, -ig, -og,* or *-ug*. (Refer to the Challenge Words list on the facing page if necessary.) Then have children make word cards for these new words. Encourage them to work in pairs or small groups to sort the words into word families. Ask them to think of one additional way to sort the Challenge Word cards.

Teacher Tip

Children having difficulty with the sort may benefit from concentrating on one word family at a time. For example, have children read through all the cards, listening for words with *-ag* before moving to another word family.

You may wish to use the Sort 25 **Build, Blend, and Extend**. (See the Teacher Resource CD.)

Sort 26

Word Families -ill, -ell, -all

Objectives

- To recognize and read words in word families *-ill*, *-ell*, and *-all*
- To identify and sort pictures and words with *-ill*, *-ell*, and *-all*

Materials

 Big Book of Rhymes, Level A, "Play Ball!," page 51

 Teacher Resource CD, Level A

 Word Study Notebook, Level A, pages 103–106

 Words Their Way Library, Level A, *Eight Friends in All*

 Teacher Resource CD, Level A, Rhyming Go Fish Game

Words			Pictures		
-ill	*-ell*	*-all*	*-ill*	*-ell*	*-all*
fill	tell	mall	mill	well	fall
will	sell	call	hill	yell	ball
still	fell	hall	sill	shell	tall

Challenge Words

-ill	*-ell*	*-all*
spill	swell	stall
grill	spell	small
skill		

Day 1 Introduce the Sort

Whole Group

 Read a Rhyme: "Play Ball!"

Read aloud the poem "Play Ball!" several times, emphasizing the rhyming words. Ask children to name words they hear in the poem that rhyme. *(ball, call, all; Bill, Jill; Nell, well, yell).* Write the words in columns on the chalkboard. Help children understand that the words rhyme because they are in the same word family. Read the poem again, omitting the last word of each line, and have children supply the missing word.

 Introduce Picture/Word Sort *-ill*, *-ell*, *-all*

Print and cut apart the picture/word cards for Sort 26 from the Teacher Resource CD. Introduce the words and pictures, and define in context words and picture names that may be unfamiliar to children, such as *yell*, *mall*, and *mill*. Then demonstrate for children how to name each picture and word and sort the cards into *-ill*, *-ell*, and *-all* word families.

Day 2 Practice the Sort

Whole Group/Independent/Partner

 You may want to begin Days 2–5 by rereading the rhyme from Day 1. Then review the previous day's sort demonstration. Help children remove page 103 from their Word Study Notebook and cut apart the cards.

Have children work independently or with a partner to say each picture and word name and, using the grid on page 105, sort the cards by word families.

> **Alternative Sort: Places or Actions**
>
> After children have had success sorting the picture and word cards, invite them to sort the cards in a different way. Set aside cards for *will*, *still*, *ball*, *tall*, and *shell*. Then have children sort the pictures and words for places *(hall, mall, hill, mill, sill, well)* and pictures and words for actions *(call, tell, sell, fill, fell, fall, yell)*. You may want to point out that some words, such as *well*, can have more than one meaning.

Find Words in Context

Whole Group

Have children re-sort their cards. Then show children the cover of the book *Eight Friends in All*. Read the title aloud, and ask children which word belongs in one of this week's word families. *(all)* Read the book with children. Have them listen for and identify the two additional words that belong in the *all* word family. *(tall, ball)* Ask children to look through their word cards to find the two picture cards that match words in the text. *(tall, ball)*

Apply the Skill

Independent/Partner

Have children sort their cards again. Then have children turn to page 106 in their Word Study Notebook. Read aloud the directions and have children work independently or with a partner to use the given letters to make five words for each word family.

Complete the Sort

Whole Group/Independent

Paste in Place

Have children turn to page 105 in their Word Study Notebook. Encourage children to say the name of each picture and word and sort their cards according to *-ill*, *-ell*, and *-all* word families. Then have them paste the cards in place on the page.

Play the Game

When children are finished, they may play the Rhyming Go Fish game (See the Teacher Resource CD for the playing cards and directions.)

Building Vocabulary

If children are only familiar with a shopping mall, describe an outdoor mall in a town or city that is like a small park. Lead children to compare the two kinds of malls and understand that a mall is usually a large area, for everyone to use, and where it is easy to move about.

ESL/ELL English Language Learners

To help children learn to discriminate among short vowel sounds, say two words, such as *tell* and *will*. Elongate each vowel sound. Have children repeat the words after you in the same way and tell whether the words have the same vowel sound. Repeat with other pairs, making sure to include word pairs from the same word family.

Challenge Words Activity

Help children brainstorm other words that end with *-ill*, *-ell*, or *-all*. Refer to the Challenge Words list, as needed. Then help children make word cards for these words. Encourage them to work in pairs or small groups to sort the words into word families. Ask children to think of another way to sort these cards.

Teacher Tip

Children may also enjoy using words in a word family to create tongue twisters, such as *Tell Nell I'll sell the shell*. This will help them to discriminate among the short *a*, *e*, and *i* vowel sounds.

You may wish to use the Sort 26 **Build, Blend, and Extend.** (See the Teacher Resource CD.)

Word Families -ick, -ack, -uck, -ock

Objectives

- To recognize and read words in word families *-ick, -ack, -uck,* and *-ock*
- To identify and sort pictures and words ending with *-ick, -ack, -uck,* or *-ock*

Materials

 Big Book of Rhymes, Level A, "Time Talk," page 53

 Teacher Resource CD, Level A

 Word Study Notebook, Level A, pages 107–110

 Words Their Way Library, Level A, *My Clock Is Sick*

 Teacher Resource CD, Level A, Word Maker Game

Words

-ick	-ack	-uck	-ock
pick	pack	buck	dock
quick	rack	luck	clock
lick	snack	cluck	rock

Pictures

sick	black	stuck	lock
kick	tack	duck	block

Challenge Words

wick	crack	pluck	shock
flick	smack	shuck	knock
slick			

Day 1 Introduce the Sort

Whole Group

 Read a Rhyme: "Time Talk"

To introduce the word families *-ick, -ack, -uck,* and *-ock,* read the poem "Time Talk." As you read, emphasize the rhyming words *(too, do; quick, tick; chime, time).* Ask children to find the rhyming pair *quick* and *tick.* Write the words in a column on the chalkboard. Ask children how the words are alike. Read the poem again, omitting the last word of each line, and have children supply the word.

 Introduce Picture/Word Sort -ick, -ack, -uck, -ock

Print and cut apart the picture/word cards for Sort 27 from the Teacher Resource CD. Introduce the words and pictures, and define in context words and picture names that may be unfamiliar to children, such as *rack, cluck,* and *buck.* Then demonstrate for children how to sort the pictures and words into *-ick, -ack, -uck,* and *-ock* word families.

Day 2 Practice the Sort

Whole Group/Independent/Partner

 You may want to begin Days 2–5 by rereading the rhyme from Day 1. Then review the previous day's sort demonstration. Help children remove page 107 from their Word Study Notebook and cut apart the cards.

Have children work independently or with a partner to say the name of each picture and word card and, using the grid on page 109, sort their cards by word families.

Alternative Sort: Ready, Set, Action

When children are comfortable with this week's sort, lead them in another sort. Discuss action words with children. Provide examples as necessary. Help children sort the cards into action words and other words. You may want to point out that some words, such as *lock,* can fit both categories. Children will enjoy performing the action words as you sort the cards.

Day 3 Find Words in Context

Whole Group

Have children re-sort their cards. Then read *My Clock Is Sick* with children. Have them listen for and identify words that end with *-ick, -ack,* or *-ock.*

Have children look through their word cards to find the two cards that match words in the text. (*sick, quick*) Then have them find other words in the story that end with *-ick, -ack,* or *-ock. (tick, Jack, tock, clock)*

Day 4 Apply the Skill

Independent/Partner

Have children sort their cards again. Then have children turn to page 110 in their Word Study Notebook. Read aloud the directions, and have children work independently or with a partner to use the letters provided to make four words for each word family.

Day 5 Complete the Sort

Whole Group/Independent

Paste in Place

Have children turn to page 109 in their Word Study Notebook. Encourage children to say the name of each picture and word, and sort their cards according to *-ick, -ack, -uck,* and *-ock* word families. Then have children paste the pictures in place on the page.

Play the Game

When children are finished, they may play the Word Maker game (See the Teacher Resource CD for the playing cards and directions.)

Building Vocabulary

Show the photograph of the tire in the mud, and emphasize that *stuck* will be used to name the action. Ask children to think of different ways this action could be shown.

ESL/ELL English Language Learners

The distinction between short *a* and short *i* may be difficult for English language learners. To help them hear the difference, say each word in the sort. Emphasize the vowel sound as you say each word.

Challenge Words Activity

Help children brainstorm other words that end with *-ick, -ack, -uck,* or *-ock.* Refer to the Challenge Words list, as necessary. Then have children make word cards for these new words. Encourage them to work in pairs or small groups to sort the words into categories.

Teacher Tip

When children complete a sort, remind them to read each word and say the name of each picture in a column to check their work. Some students may find it helpful to trace each of the three word family endings using a different color crayon or marker. If children respond to this technique, you may consider color coding the word cards you use in the Day 1 activity.

You may wish to use the Sort 27 **Build, Blend, and Extend.** (See the Teacher Resource CD.)

Word Families -ish, -ash, -ush

Objectives

- To recognize and read words in word families *-ish*, *-ash*, and *-ush*
- To identify and sort words with *-ish*, *-ash*, or *-ush*

Materials

 Big Book of Rhymes, Level A, "Dinnertime," page 55

 Teacher Resource CD, Level A

 Word Study Notebook, Level A, pages 111–114

 Words Their Way Library, Level A, *Something to Munch*

 Teacher Resource CD, Level A, Pick a Dish Game

Words		
-ish	*-ash*	*-ush*
dish	crash	blush
swish	dash	crush
wish	flash	flush
	mash	hush
	rash	mush
	smash	plush
	trash	rush

Challenge Words

gash	gush
clash	lush
slash	

Day 1 — Introduce the Sort

Whole Group

 Read a Rhyme: "Dinnertime"

Introduce word families *-ish*, *-ash*, and *-ush* by reading the poem "Dinnertime." As you read, emphasize the end rhymes *(rush, crush; dish, fish; crash, trash)*. As children find the rhyming words in the poem, write them in three columns on the board or on chart paper. Then ask children how the words are alike. *(They rhyme and end with the same sounds.)* Read the poem again, omitting the last word of each line, and have children supply the word.

 Introduce Word Sort *-ish*, *-ash*, *-ush*

Print and cut apart the word cards for Sort 28 from the Teacher Resource CD. Introduce the words, and define in context words that may be unfamiliar to children, such as *swish*, *hush*, *mush*, and *plush*. Then demonstrate how to sort the words into *-ish*, *-ash*, and *-ush* word families. Encourage children to read aloud the words in each column and tell how they are alike.

Day 2 — Practice the Sort

Whole Group/Independent/Partner

 You may want to begin Days 2–5 by rereading the rhyme from Day 1. Then review the previous day's sort demonstration. Help children remove page 111 from their Word Study Notebook and cut apart the word cards.

Have children work independently or with a partner to say the words and, using the grid on page 113, sort the word cards by word families. Have children read the words as they work.

> **Alternative Sort: Beginning Sound Sort**
>
> After children have been successful with this week's sort, invite them to sort the cards into words that begin with an initial consonant blend and words that begin with only one initial consonant.

Find Words in Context

Whole Group

Have children re-sort their cards. Then have children listen for words that end with *-ish* or *-ash* as you read the book *Something to Munch*. After reading, ask children to look through their word cards to find cards that match words in the text. (*dish, mash, crash*) Then have children find another word in the story that belongs in the *-ash* word family. (*bash*) Children may identify the word *wash*. Point out that although it has the same ending letters as the *-ash* words in the sort, it is pronounced differently.

Apply the Skill

Independent/Partner

Have children sort their cards again. Then have children turn to page 114 in their Word Study Notebook. Read aloud the directions, and have children work independently or with a partner to use the given letters to make five words for each word family.

Complete the Sort

Whole Group/Independent

Paste in Place

Have children turn to page 113 in their Word Study Notebook. Encourage children to say the name of each word and sort their cards according to *-ish*, *-ash*, and *-ush* word families. Then have them paste the pictures in place on the page.

Play the Game

When children are finished, they may play the Pick a Dish game. (See the Teacher Resource CD for the game board, spinner, rhyming words sheet, and directions.)

Building Vocabulary

Use *swish* in a sentence as a noun, but explain that *swish* can be an object, action, or sound. Model for the class how to use *swish* in a sentence with the other meanings. Then invite children to use *swish* in sentences and tell what it means in each.

ESL/ELL English Language Learners

Children benefit from learning new words in context. When introducing the words for this week's sort, use each word in context. Then engage children in speaking activities. Have them repeat the word and your sample sentence, and then use the word in a sentence of their own.

Challenge Words Activity

Help children brainstorm other words that end with *ash* or *ush*. Refer to the Challenge Words list on the facing page if necessary. Then have children make word cards for these new words. Encourage them to work in pairs or small groups to sort the words into word families. Ask them to think of one additional way to sort the Challenge Word cards.

Teacher Tip

Continue to help children build automaticity as they sort. After each sort, have children read the words in each column as quickly as they can.

You may wish to use the Sort 28 **Build, Blend, and Extend.** (See the Teacher Resource CD.)

Spell Check 4

After completing Sorts 22–28, you may want to administer Spell Check 4 in the Word Study Notebook on page 158. See page 19 for instructions on assessment.

Objectives

- To identify short vowels *a* and *o*
- To identify and sort pictures and words with short vowels *a* and *o*

Materials

 Big Book of Rhymes, Level A, "Jogging", page 57

 Teacher Resource CD, Level A

 Word Study Notebook, Level A, pages 115–118

 Words Their Way Library, Level A, *The Ant*

 Teacher Resource CD, Level A, Ant Trek Game

Words		Pictures	
ă	ŏ	ă	ŏ
had	job	bag	sock
jam	hot	can	lock
ran	got	cap	rock
hat	top	jack	mop
ham	jog	bat	box
van	log	grass	clock

Challenge Words

ă	ŏ
man	shop
has	chop
fast	block
back	drop

Day 1

Introduce the Sort

Whole Group

 ### Read a Rhyme: "Jogging"

Read the poem "Jogging." As you read, emphasize the words that contain the sounds of short *a* and *o*. (*ant, jog, ran, fog, trot, hot, sat, log*) Ask children to name the words they hear in the poem with the short vowel sounds of *a* and *o*. Write the words in two columns on the chalkboard or on chart paper. Help children understand that the words in each column contain the same short vowel sound.

 ### Introduce Picture/Word Sort Short Vowels *a, o*

Print and cut apart the cards for Sort 29 from the Teacher Resource CD. Introduce the words, and define in context words that may be unfamiliar, such as *jam, log,* and *had.* Then demonstrate how to say the name of each picture, and sort the cards by the short vowel *a* and *o* sounds. Ask children to describe how the pictures in each column are alike. Then have children sort the word cards by vowel sounds.

Day 2

Practice the Sort

Whole Group/Independent/Partner

 You may want to begin Days 2–5 by rereading the rhyme from Day 1. Then review the previous day's sort demonstration. Help children tear out page 115 from their Word Study Notebook and cut apart the word and picture cards.

Have children work independently or with a partner to say the name of each picture and word and, using the grid on page 117 in their Word Study Notebook, sort the picture cards and word cards by short *a* and short *o* vowel sounds.

Alternative Sort: Will It Fit?

Have children re-sort the words and pictures into two categories: things that would usually fit into a backpack (*jam, top, hat, ham, sock, bag, lock, rock, can, cap, jack, box, grass, clock*) and things that would not (*log, mop, van, bat*). Before beginning the sort, set aside the word cards *had, job, hot, ran, got,* and *jog.*

Day 3

Find Words in Context

Whole Group /Independent

Have children re-sort their cards. Then read the book *The Ant* with children. After several readings, have children listen for and identify words with the short vowel sounds of *a* or *o*.

Have children look through their word cards to find words that match words in the text. Then have them find other words in the story that include the short vowel sounds *a* or *o*.

Day 4

Apply the Skill

Independent/Partner

Have children sort their cards again. Then have children turn to page 118 in their Word Study Notebook. Read aloud the directions and encourage children to work independently or with a partner to write words that contain the short vowel sounds of *a* or *o*.

Day 5

Complete the Sort

Whole Group/Independent

Paste in Place

Have children turn to page 117 in their Word Study Notebook. Encourage them to sort and match their pictures and words by short *a* and short *o* vowel sounds. Then have them paste the pictures in place on the page.

Play the Game

When children are finished, they may play the Ant Trek game. (See the Teacher Resource CD for the game board, spinner, and directions.)

Building Vocabulary

Show children the picture card for *jack* and explain that this small metal piece with six points or prongs is used in playing the game of jacks. Invite volunteers to demonstrate how to play the game.

ESL/ELL English Language Learners

Review the pictures and words with children. Emphasize action words that contain short *a* or *o* vowel sounds *(ran, jog)* by having children act out the motions associated with each word.

Challenge Words Activity

Ask children to find other words that include the short vowel sounds *a* or *o*. If children need prompting, make suggestions from the Challenge Words list. Then have children make word cards for these new words. They can work in small groups to sort the words into categories.

Teacher Tip

During the second or a repeated sort, do not correct children when they place a picture or word in the wrong column. Wait until they have completed the sort, and have them read the words in each column to check them. If children still do not find the misplaced picture or word, tell them which column it is in, and have them find it.

Sort 30

Short Vowels *i, u*

Objectives

- To identify short vowels *i* and *u*
- To identify and sort pictures and words with the short vowel sounds *i* or *u*

Materials

Big Book of Rhymes, Level A, "Having Fun," page 59

Teacher Resource CD, Level A

Word Study Notebook, Level A, pages 119–122

Words Their Way Library, Level A, *Just Like Us*

Teacher Resource CD, Level A, Fishing Fun Game

Words		Pictures	
ĭ	ŭ	ĭ	ŭ
zip	but	fin	sun
sit	cup	bib	cut
tin	hum	lid	nut
rip	jug	wig	bug
big	bun	pig	bus
fig	tub	fish	duck

Challenge Words

ĭ	ŭ
with	must
grin	such
still	jump
miss	crust

Day 1 Introduce the Sort

Whole Group

Read a Rhyme: "Having Fun"

Read the poem "Having Fun." After several readings, emphasize the words that contain the short vowel sounds *i* or *u*. (*run, fun, big, ship, trip, wig, jig*) Ask children to listen and name the words they hear in the poem that have the sound of short *i* or *u*. Write these words in two columns on the chalkboard or on chart paper. Help children understand that the words in each column contain the same vowel sound.

Introduce Picture/Word Sort Short Vowels *i, u*

Print and cut apart the picture/word cards for Sort 30 from the Teacher Resource CD. Introduce the words and pictures, and define in context names that may be unfamiliar to children, such as *tin, fig,* and *hum*. Then demonstrate for children how to say each picture name or word and sort the pictures by short *i* and short *u* vowel sounds. Ask children to describe how the pictures in each column are alike. Then have children sort the word cards by vowel sounds.

Day 2 Practice the Sort

Whole Group/Independent/Partner

You may want to begin Days 2–5 by rereading the rhyme from Day 1. Then review the previous day's sort demonstration. Help children remove page 119 from their Word Study Notebook and cut apart the word and picture cards.

Have children work independently or with a partner to say the name of each picture and word and, using the grid on page 121 of their Word Study Notebook, sort the cards by short *i* and short *u* vowel sounds.

Alternative Sort: Indoors or Outdoors

When children are comfortable with this week's sort, remove all cards that are not names or pictures of objects or things. Then have students re-sort the word cards and pictures cards based on whether the objects named or pictured can usually be seen outdoors or indoors.

Day 3

Find Words in Context

Whole Group /Independent/Partner

Have children re-sort their cards. Then read the book *Just Like Us* with children. Have children listen for and identify any words that include the short vowel sounds *i* or *u*.

Have children look through their word cards to find words that match words in the text. Then have them find other words in the story that include the short vowel sounds *i* or *u*.

Day 4

Apply the Skill

Independent/Partner

Have children sort their cards again. Then have children turn to page 122 in their Word Study Notebook. Read aloud the directions and encourage children to work independently or with a partner to write words that contain the short vowel sounds *i* or *u*.

Day 5

Complete the Sort

Whole Group/Independent

Paste in Place

Have children turn to page 121 in their Word Study Notebook. Encourage them to sort and match their pictures and words into groups of short *i* and short *u* vowel sounds. Then have them paste the pictures and matching words in place on the page.

Play the Game

When children are finished, they may play the Fishing Fun game. (See the Teacher Resource CD for the game board, playing cards, and directions.)

Building Vocabulary

If children are not familiar with what tin is, explain that this kind of metal is used to make containers such as cans, roofs, and toys. Encourage them to find items around the classroom that are made of tin.

ESL/ELL English Language Learners

Pair proficient and nonproficient English speakers. Have the pairs re-sort the pictures and words into groups of short *i* and short *u* vowel sounds, saying the words and picture names aloud together.

Challenge Words Activity

Ask children to find other words that include the short vowel sounds *i* or *u*. If children need prompting, make suggestions from the Challenge Words list. Then have children make word cards for these new words. They can work in small groups to sort the words into categories.

Teacher Tip

When children are comfortable with this week's sort, have them repeat the sort with an emphasis on speed. To this end, have children with similar aptitudes work in pairs to race each other to re-sort the words from their Word Study Notebook into short *i* and short *u* vowel sounds.

Short Vowels e, i, o, u

Objectives

- To identify short vowels *e*, *i*, *o*, and *u*
- To identify and sort pictures and words with short vowels *e*, *i*, *o*, or *u*

Materials

 Big Book of Rhymes, Level A, "Nighttime," page 61

 Teacher Resource CD, Level A

 Word Study Notebook, Level A, pages 123–126

 Words Their Way Library, Level A, *Night and Day*

 Teacher Resource CD, Level A, Star Trip Game

Words

ĕ	ĭ	ŏ	ŭ
wet	hid	hot	cub
ten	bin	fog	sun
den	his	not	rut

Pictures

bed	chin	hop	rug
sled	brick	pot	nut

Challenge Words

desk	clip	lock	just
steps	spill	frock	skunk
best	brink	crop	brush

Day 1 Introduce the Sort

Whole Group

 Read a Rhyme: "Nighttime"

Read the poem "Nighttime," and emphasize the words that contain short *e*, *i*, *o*, or *u* vowel sounds (*setting, hen, rest, nest, will, chicks, trot, spot, soft, sun, upon*). Ask children to name the words they hear in the poem that have short *e*, *i*, *o*, or *u* vowel sounds. Write the words in four columns on the chalkboard or on chart paper. Help children understand that the words in each column have the same short vowel sound.

 Introduce Picture/Word Sort Short Vowels e, i, o, u

Whole Group

Print and cut apart the picture/word cards for Sort 31 from the Teacher Resource CD. Introduce the words and pictures, and define in context words and picture names that may be unfamiliar to children, such as *bin, cub, rut,* and *hop*. Then demonstrate how to sort the pictures and words into short *e*, *i*, *o*, and *u* vowel sounds. Have children describe how the pictures and words in each column are alike.

Day 2 Practice the Sort

Whole Group/Independent/Partner

 You may want to begin Days 2–5 by rereading the rhyme from Day 1. Then review the previous day's sort demonstration. Help children tear out page 123 from their Word Study Notebook and cut apart the cards.

Have children work independently or with a partner to say the name of each picture and word and, using the grid on page 125 of their Word Study Notebook, sort the cards by their short vowel sound.

Alternative Sort: Rhyming Sort

When children are comfortable with this week's sort, display the word and picture cards. Ask children to re-sort the words to make rhyming pairs. For example, children would sort *hot, pot,* and *nut, rut.* Tell children that not all cards will have a rhyming match. After the sort, have children read the pairs that rhyme.

Day 3 — Find Words in Context

Whole Group /Independent/Partner

Have children re-sort their cards. Then read the book *Night and Day* with children. Have children listen for and identify any words that include the short vowel sounds *e, i, o,* or *u.*

Have children look through their word cards to find words that match words in the text. Then have them find other words in the story that include the short vowel sounds *e, i, o,* or *u.*

Day 4 — Apply the Skill

Independent/Partner

Have children sort their cards again. Then have children turn to page 126 in their Word Study Notebook. Read aloud the directions, and encourage children to work independently or with a partner to write words that contain the short *e, i, o,* or *u* vowel sounds.

Day 5 — Complete the Sort

Whole Group/Independent

Paste in Place

Have children turn to page 125 in their Word Study Notelbook. Encourage children to say the name of each picture and word and sort the cards into short *e, i, o,* or *u* vowel sounds. Then have them paste the pictures in place on the page.

Play the Game

When children are finished, they may play the Star Trip game. (See the Teacher Resource CD for the game board, spinner, and directions.)

Building Vocabulary

Children may use different words for *bin*. Check that they understand that a bin is a storage container and then talk about what people store in bins. Children might mention recycling materials, vegetables, firewood, and things for sale in a store.

ESL/ELL English Language Learners

Review the pictures and words with children. Then pair children with native English speakers to help them read and understand the words and their meanings.

Challenge Words Activity

Ask children to find other words that include the short vowel sounds *e, i, o,* or *u.* If children need prompting, make suggestions from the Challenge Words. Then have children make word cards for these new words. Children can work in small groups to sort the words into categories.

Teacher Tip

To help children understand relationships, have children sort objects such as buttons, pencils, and so on, and tell why they made the sorts that they did. Encourage children to think of different ways to sort the objects.

Words With Beginning Consonant Digraphs and Short Vowels a, e, i

Objectives

- To identify short *a*, *e*, and *i* vowel sounds in words beginning with consonant digraphs
- To identify and sort words with beginning consonant digraphs and short vowel *a*, *e*, or *i*

Materials

 Big Book of Rhymes, Level A, "The Treasure Chest," page 63

 Teacher Resource CD, Level A

 Word Study Notebook, Level A, pages 127-130

 Words Their Way Library, Level A, *Stan Packs*

 Teacher Resource CD, Level A, Word Maker Game

Words

ă	ĕ	ĭ
that	them	thick
chat	shed	thin
than	then	whip
chap	chest	chill
shack	shell	ship
wham	check	chick
shall	when	whiz

Challenge Words

chant	shelf	this
whack	chess	which
what		shin
thank		whisk

Day 1

Introduce the Sort

Whole Group

 Read a Rhyme: "The Treasure Chest"

Introduce short *a*, *e*, and *i* vowel sounds in words that begin with consonant digraphs by reading the poem "The Treasure Chest." As you read, emphasize words with these sounds. *(Chen, chest, what's, ship, then, shell, thinks)* Help children understand that these words contain short vowel sounds and initial consonant digraphs.

 Introduce Word Sort Words With Beginning Consonant Digraphs and Short Vowels a, e, i

Whole Group

Print and cut apart the word cards for Sort 32 from the Teacher Resource CD. Introduce the words, and define in context words that may be unfamiliar to children, such as *than*, *wham*, and *whiz*. Then demonstrate for children how to sort the words into short *a*, *e*, and *i* vowel sounds. Ask children to describe how the words in each column are alike.

Day 2

Practice the Sort

Whole Group/Independent/Partner

 You may want to begin Days 2–5 by rereading the rhyme from Day 1. Then review the previous day's word sort demonstration. Help children tear out page 127 from their Word Study Notebook and cut apart the word cards.

Have children work independently or with a partner to say each word and, using the grid on page 129, sort the cards by their short vowel sounds.

> **Alternative Sort: Beginning Sounds**
> When children are comfortable with this week's sort, ask them to sort the words by beginning digraph.

Day 3

Find Words in Context

Whole Group /Independent/Partner

Have children re-sort their cards. Then read the book *Stan Packs* with children. Have children listen for and identify any words that begin with consonant digraphs and include the short vowel sounds *a*, *e*, or *i*.

Day 4

Apply the Skill

Independent/Partner

Have children sort their cards again. Then have children turn to page 130 in their Word Study Notebook. Read aloud the directions, and encourage children to work independently or with a partner to write words that contain short vowels *a*, *e*, or *i*.

Day 5

Complete the Sort

Whole Group/Independent

Paste in Place

Have children turn to page 129 in their Word Study Notebook. Encourage children to say each word and sort the cards by their short vowel sound. Then have them paste the words in place on the page.

Play the Game

When children are finished, they may play the Word Maker game. (See the Teacher Resource CD for the playing cards and directions.)

Building Vocabulary

Clarify that *shall* means "do in the future," and say, "You shall go home at [time]." Have children finish several sentences you begin with "You shall ___," "We shall ___," and "I shall ___."

ESL/ELL English Language Learners

Help children pronounce and distinguish between the beginning sound of *th* in *thick* and *them*. Ask them to repeat each word after you, and listen to make sure that they are pronouncing the words correctly.

Challenge Words Activity

Ask children to find other short vowel *a*, *e*, or *i* words that contain beginning consonant digraphs. If children need prompting, make suggestions from the Challenge Words List. Then have children make word cards for these new words. They can work in small groups to sort the words into categories.

Teacher Tip

Extend practice of the skill by having children go on a word hunt to find words in books that begin with the target sound. Tell children to copy the words they find on cards. Then have children pool and sort their words by short vowel sound and then by initial consonant digraphs.

Objectives

- To identify words with beginning blends and short vowels
- To identify and sort words with short vowels and beginning blends

Materials

 Big Book of Rhymes, Level A, "Greg Packs," page 65

 Teacher Resource CD, Level A

 Word Study Notebook, Level A, pages 131–134

 Words Their Way Library, Level A, *Roll Out the Red Rug*

 Teacher Resource CD, Level A, Word Maker Game

Words

ă	ĕ	ĭ	ŏ	ŭ
flag	bled	slid	slob	fluff
glad	fret	drip	flop	gruff
slap	dress	clip	trot	plug
flat	sled	drill	gloss	truck
crab	fled	spin	plot	slug

Challenge Words

clan	sped	skit	blob	smug
snap	stem	spit	glob	snug
stab	step	skill	crop	spun
swam	spell	trip	spot	stub

Day 1 — Introduce the Sort

Whole Group

 Read a Rhyme: "Greg Packs"

Introduce short vowel words with beginning blends by reading the poem "Greg Packs." As you read, emphasize the words with the target skill. (*Greg, plans, trip, thing, from, skip, trunk, sled, stuff, crushes, spot, brushes*) Ask children to identify words that have the target sounds. Write them in five columns on the chalkboard or on chart paper. Ask children how the words in each column are alike.

 Introduce Word Sort Short Vowel Words With Beginning Blends

Whole Group

Print and cut apart the word cards for Sort 33 from the Teacher Resource CD. Introduce the words, and define in context words that may be unfamiliar to children, such as *bled, fled, fret, slob, gloss,* and *gruff.* Then demonstrate how to sort the words into short *a, e, i, o,* and *u* vowel sounds. Ask children to describe how the words in each column are alike.

Day 2 — Practice the Sort

Whole Group/Independent

 You may want to begin Days 2–5 by rereading the rhyme from Day 1. Then review the previous day's sort demonstration. Help children remove page 131 from their Word Study Notebook and cut apart the word cards.

Have children work independently or with a partner to say each word and, using the grid on page 133 in their Word Study Notebook, sort the cards by their short vowel sound.

> **Alternative Sort: Beginning Blends**
>
> When children are comfortable with this week's sort, have them work in pairs to sort the words according to *l* blends (*slob, slop, bled, flag, fluff, gloss, glad, slap, plot, sled, flat, slug, fled*) and *r* blends (*trot, fret, gruff, dress, drip, drill, crab*). Then have children sort the *l* blend words into *sl, bl, fl, gl,* and *pl* groups, and the *r* blend words into *tr, fr, gr, dr,* and *cr* groups.

Day 3

Find Words in Context

Whole Group /Independent/Partner

Have children re-sort their cards. Then read the book *Roll Out the Red Rug* with children. Have children listen for any words that begin with a blend and contain a short vowel sound. Then have children look for and identify words in the story that begin with a digraph and have the short vowel sound.

Day 4

Apply the Skill

Independent/Partner

Have children sort their cards again. Then have children turn to page 134 in their Word Study Notebook. Read aloud the directions, and encourage children to work independently or with a partner to write write the words under their correct short vowel sound.

Day 5

Complete the Sort

Whole Group/Independent

Paste in Place

Have children turn to page 133 in their Word Study Notebook. Encourage children to say each word and sort their cards by short vowel sounds. Then have them paste the words in place on the page.

Play the Game

When children are finished, they may play the Word Maker game. (See Teacher Resource CD for the playing cards and directions.)

Building Vocabulary

Ask children what *fled* means, and make sure they understand it means "ran away or escaped from danger or from something unpleasant." Have volunteers take turns using *fled* in a sentence for the group to repeat.

ESL/ELL English Language Learners

Review the word cards with children. You may need to place special emphasis on the pronunciation of words that contain beginning blends. If possible, try to set aside time to work individually with children to help them pronounce words that contain difficult or unfamiliar sounds.

Challenge Words Activity

Ask children to find other words that begin with digraphs and contain a short vowel sound. If children need prompting, make suggestions from the Challenge Words List. Then have children make word cards for these new words. They can work in small groups to sort the words into categories.

Teacher Tip

When you assign children to work together in small groups to complete an activity, you may want to choose one child to be the moderator. That child comes to you with questions or concerns the group might have.

Sort 34

Short Vowel Words With Final Blends

Objectives

- To identify short vowel words with final blends
- To identify and sort words with short vowels and final blends

Materials

 Big Book of Rhymes, Level A, "My Cow," page 67

 Teacher Resource CD, Level A

 Word Study Notebook, Level A, pages 135–138

 Words Their Way Library, Level A, *That Pig Can't Do a Thing*

 Teacher Resource CD, Level A, Bingo! Game

Words

ă	ě	ĭ	ŏ	ŭ
mask	melt	list	lost	just
fast	desk	fist	soft	must
raft	best	gift	cost	tusk
past	nest	milk		dust
half	left	lift		husk

Challenge Words

cast	rest	disk	frost	trust
task	test	sift		bulk
blast	crest	swift		

Day 1 — Introduce the Sort

Whole Group

Read a Rhyme: "My Cow"

Introduce short vowel sounds in words with final blends by reading the poem "My Cow." As you read, emphasize the words with final blends that contain short vowel sounds *(best, stands, rest, pink, soft, rump, jump, milk)*. Help children understand that each of these words contains a short vowel sound and a final blend. Read the poem several times, inviting children to join in.

Introduce Word Sort Short Vowel Words With Final Blends

Whole Group

Print and cut apart the word cards for Sort 34 from the Teacher Resource CD. Introduce the words, and define in context words that may be unfamiliar to children, such as *tusk, husk,* and *raft.* Then demonstrate for children how to sort the words into short vowel *a, e, i, o,* and *u* sounds. Ask children to describe how the words in each column are alike. *(They contain short vowel sounds and final blends.)*

Day 2 — Practice the Sort

Whole Group/Independent/Partner

You may want to begin Days 2–5 by rereading the rhyme from Day 1. Then review the previous day's sort demonstration. Help children remove page 135 from their Word Study Notebook and cut apart the cards.

Using the grid on page 137 of their Word Study Notebook, have children work independently or with a partner to say each word and sort the word cards into short *a, e, i, o,* and *u* vowel sounds.

Alternative Sort: What Can You Give Me?

When children are comfortable with this week's sort, ask them to re-sort the words into two categories—words that describe something you could give to another person and words that don't fit that category. After the sort has been made, ask children to read the sort and give reasons for their choices.

Day 3 Find Words in Context

Whole Group /Independent

 Have children re-sort their cards. Then read the book *That Pig Can't Do a Thing* with children. Have them listen for words that contain the short vowel sounds *a, e, i, o,* or *u.*

Day 4 Apply the Skill

Independent/Partner

 Have children sort their cards again. Then have children turn to page 138 in their Word Study Notebook. Read aloud the directions and encourage children to work independently or with a partner to say each word and print the word in the box that shows its vowel sound.

Day 5 Complete the Sort

Whole Group/Independent

Paste in Place

 Have children turn to page 137 in their Word Study Notebook. Encourage children to sort and match their words into the short vowel sounds *a, e, i, o,* and *u.* Then have them paste the cards in place on the page.

Play the Game

When children are finished, they may play the Bingo! game. (See the Teacher Resource CD for the game board, playing cards, and directions.)

Building Vocabulary

Model using *best* versus *good* and *better* by showing one of three books and saying, "I think this story is good." Continue showing and saying which is better and the best of all. Have children use three books or other objects to explain their opinions with *good, better,* and *best.*

ESL/ELL English Language Learners

Review the words with children. Emphasize the pronunciation of the final blends. Have children pronounce each word to be sure they are able to correctly pronounce difficult final blends. During a group sort, you may wish to pair children who need help with proficient English speakers.

Challenge Words Activity

Ask children to find other words with a short vowel and a final blend. If children need prompting, make suggestions from the Challenge Words list. Then have children make word cards for these new words. They can work in small groups to sort the words into categories.

Teacher Tip

Some children may benefit from drawing pictures to match the word cards. Have volunteers share their pictures.

Sort 35

Short Vowels a, e, i, o, u

Objectives

- To identify words with short vowel sounds
- To identify and sort words with short vowel sounds

Materials

Big Book of Rhymes, Level A, "The Trip," page 69

Teacher Resource CD, Level A

Word Study Notebook, Level A, pages 139–142

Words Their Way Library, Level A, *The Trip*

Teacher Resource CD, Level A, Let's Shop Game

Words

ă	ĕ	ĭ	ŏ	ŭ
mask	shed	quick	cloth	gruff
jack	check	chick	fox	truck
cat	desk	grill	moth	drum
shack	nest	pig	toss	bus
flag	sled	ship	cross	club

Challenge Words

clash	blend	blink	loss	stunt
crush	fresh	drink	gloss	slump
champ	drench	sling	slot	brush
	spent			blush

Day 1 — Introduce the Sort

Whole Group

Read a Rhyme: "The Trip"

Read aloud the poem "The Trip." As you read, emphasize words that contain short vowel sounds. *(Meg, Dan, on, trip, shop, skip, gets, cat, Scat, hat, then, stop, bun, lots, fun)* Ask children to name words they hear that have short vowel sounds. Write them in five columns on the chalkboard or on chart paper. Help children understand that these words contain short vowel sounds.

Introduce Word Sort Short Vowels a, e, i, o, u

Whole Group

Print and cut apart the word cards for Sort 35 from the Teacher Resource CD. Introduce the words, and define in context words that may be unfamiliar to children, such as *shack, shed,* and *gruff* and multiple meanings of *grill, cross,* and *drum*. Then demonstrate for children how to sort the words by short vowel sounds. Ask children to describe how the words in each column are alike. *(They have the same short vowel sound.)*

Day 2 — Practice the Sort

Whole Group/Independent/Partner

You may want to begin Days 2–5 by rereading the rhyme from Day 1. Then review the previous day's sort demonstration. Help children remove page 139 from their Word Study Notebook and cut apart the cards.

Have children work independently or with a partner to say each word and, using the grid on page 141 of their Word Study Notebook, sort the words by short vowel sound.

Alternative Sort: Identify My Category

When children are comfortable with this week's sort, re-sort the pictures or words into groups of animals and non-animals. Begin by sorting two or three of the pictures and words into the categories. When you show the next word card, invite children to identify where it will go. Continue until all the cards have been sorted.

Day 3

Find Words in Context

Whole Group/Independent/Partner

Have children re-sort their cards. Then read the book *The Trip* with children. Have children listen for and identify any words with short vowel sounds.

Have children look through their word cards to find words that match words in the text. Then have them find other words in the story that contain short vowel sounds.

Day 4

Apply the Skill

Independent/Partner

Have children sort their cards again. Then have children turn to page 142 in their Word Study Notebook. Read aloud the directions, and encourage children to work independently or with a partner to write words that contain each short vowel sound.

Day 5

Complete the Sort

Whole Group/Independent

Paste in Place

Have children turn to page 141 in their Word Study Notebook. Encourage them to read each word and sort the cards by their short vowel sound. Then have them paste the cards in place on the page.

Play the Game

When children are finished, they may play the Let's Shop game. (See the Teacher Resource CD for game board, spinner, and directions.)

Building Vocabulary

Remind children that some words can mean either the name of a thing or an action. Model for children how to make sentences, first with the noun *drum* and then with the action word *drum*. Have volunteers take turns using *drum* in sentences.

ESL/ELL English Language Learners

Review the words with children. Emphasize animal words that contain short vowel sounds (*cat, pig, frog, fox*) by acting out motions or sounds associated with each animal. Have children mimic your actions as they pronounce the words.

Challenge Words Activity

Ask children to find other words that include a short vowel sound. If children need prompting, make suggestions from the Challenge Words list. Then have children make word cards for these new words. They can work in small groups to sort the words into categories.

Teacher Tip

To extend the lesson, you might ask children to identify who in the class has a first name that contains a short vowel sound. If no names fit this category, help children think of names that do, such as *Jack, Sam, Beth, Kim, Bob, Gus,* and so on. Write the names on the chalkboard.

 Spell Check 5

After completing Sorts 29–35, you may want to administer Spell Check 5 in the Word Study Notebook on page 159. See page 19 for instructions on assessment.

Sort 36

Long Vowels a, i

Objectives

- To identify long vowels *a* and *i*
- To identify and sort picture names with long vowels *a* or *i*

Materials

  Big Book of Rhymes, Level A, "Grapes," page 71

  Teacher Resource CD, Level A

  Word Study Notebook, Level A, pages 143–146

  Words Their Way Library, Level A, *The Apple Farm*

  Teacher Resource CD, Level A, Follow the Grapevine Game

Pictures

ā	ī
rake	vine
train	prize
skate	kite
frame	smile
snake	bike
rain	hive
cape	slide
gate	dime

Day 1 — Introduce the Sort

Whole Group

  Read a Rhyme: "Grapes"

Introduce long *a* and *i* vowel sounds by reading the poem "Grapes." Emphasize the words that contain long *a* and *i*. *(grapes, plate, ate; vine, ripe, fine)* Help children understand that these words contain long vowel sounds. Read the poem again, omitting the last word of each line, and have children supply the missing word.

  Introduce Picture Sort Long Vowels *a*, *i*

Whole Group

Print and cut apart the picture cards for Sort 36 from the Teacher Resource CD. Introduce the pictures, and define in context picture names that may be unfamiliar to children, such as *prize, hive,* and *dime.* Then demonstrate for children how to sort the pictures into long *a* and *i* vowel sounds. Ask children to describe how the pictures in each column are alike. *(They contain long vowel sounds.)*

Day 2 — Practice the Sort

Whole Group/Independent/Partner

  You may want to begin Days 2–5 by rereading the rhyme from Day 1. Then review the previous day's sort demonstration. Help children remove page 143 from their Word Study Notebook and cut apart the cards.

Have children work independently or with a partner to say each picture name and, using the grid on page 145 of their Word Study Notebook, sort the words by their long vowel sound.

Alternative Sort: Identify My Category

Re-sort the pictures into groups of things that can move and things that cannot move. Begin by sorting two or three of the pictures into the categories. When you show the next picture card, invite children to identify where it will go. Continue to do this until all the cards have been sorted and children are able to guess the categories.

Day 3 — Find Words in Context

Whole Group /Independent

Have children re-sort their cards. Then read the book *The Apple Farm* with children. Have children listen for and identify any words that contain the long vowel sound *a* or *i*.

Have children look through their picture cards to find names that match words in the text. Then have them find other words in the story that include the long vowel sound *a* or *i*.

Day 4 — Apply the Skill

Independent/Partner

Have children sort their cards again. Then have children turn to page 146 in their Word Study Notebook. Read aloud the directions, and encourage children to work independently or with a partner to draw pictures of things whose names contain the long vowel sound *a* or *i*.

Day 5 — Complete the Sort

Whole Group/Independent

Paste in Place

Have children turn to page 145 in their Word Study Notebook. Encourage children to say each picture name and sort the cards into long *a* and long *i* vowel sounds. Then have them paste the pictures in place on the page.

Play the Game

When children are finished, they may play the Follow the Grapevine game (See the Teacher Resource CD for the game board, spinner, and directions.)

Building Vocabulary

Show the photograph of the blue ribbon, and emphasize that *prize* will be used to name this object. Ask children if they have ever been awarded a prize and what it looked like. Encourage them to list other things that could be shown for this word.

ESL/ELL English Language Learners

Have children work with a proficient English speaker to say the name of each picture and sort the cards by their long vowel sound. Have them work together to form sentences using the picture names.

Teacher Tip

During the second or a repeated sort, do not correct children when they place a picture in the wrong column. Wait until they have completed the sort and have them read the names of the pictures in each column to check them. If they still do not find the misplaced picture, tell them what column it is in and have them find it.

Long Vowels e, o, u

Objectives

- To identify long vowels *e*, *o*, and *u*
- To identify and sort pictures names with long vowels *e*, *o*, or *u*

Materials

Big Book of Rhymes, Level A, "Mr. Green," page 71

Teacher Resource CD, Level A

Word Study Notebook, Level A, pages 147–150

Words Their Way Library, Level A, *Mr. Wink*

Teacher Resource CD, Level A, Birdhouse Game

Pictures

ē	ō	ū
bean	road	June
dream	hose	fruit
tree	nose	mule
jeans	soap	glue
feet	goat	tube

Day 1 — Introduce the Sort

Whole Group

Read a Rhyme: "Mr. Green"

Introduce long vowels *e*, *o*, and *u* by reading the poem "Mr. Green." Emphasize the words that contain long *e*, *o*, or *u* vowel sounds (*June, tune, Green, sleep, cheep, rose, doze*). Ask children to identify words with the target sounds. Help children understand that these words contain long vowel sounds. Read the poem again, omitting the last word of each line, and have children supply the missing word.

Introduce Picture Sort
Long Vowels e, o, u

Whole Group

Print and cut apart the picture cards for Sort 37 from the Teacher Resource CD. Introduce the pictures, and define in context picture names that may be unfamiliar to children, such as *tube*, *mule*, and *goat*. Then demonstrate for children how to sort the pictures by long *e*, *o*, and *u* vowel sounds. Ask children to describe how the pictures in each column are alike.

Day 2 — Practice the Sort

Whole Group/Independent/Partner

You may want to begin Days 2–5 by rereading the rhyme from Day 1. Then review the previous day's sort demonstration. Help children remove page 147 from their Word Study Notebook and cut apart the picture cards.

Have children work independently or with a partner to say the name of each picture and, using the grid on page 149 in their Word Study Notebook, sort the cards by long *e*, *o*, and *u* sounds.

Alternative Sort: Word Hunt

When children are comfortable with this week's sort, display the cards, and ask children to suggest new ways the cards might be sorted. For example, cards might be sorted by initial consonant sounds or letters, or by final consonant sounds or letters. Have children read the words aloud after each sort has been completed.

Day 3

Find Words in Context

Whole Group/Independent/Partner

Have children re-sort their cards. Then read the book *Mr. Wink* with children. Have children listen for and identify any words that include the long vowel sounds *e*, *o*, or *u*.

Have children look through their picture cards to find names that match words in the text. Then have them find other words in the story with the long vowel sounds *e*, *o*, or *u*.

Day 4

Apply the Skill

Independent/Partner

Have children sort their cards again. Then have children turn to page 150 in their Word Study Notebook. Read aloud the directions and encourage children to work independently or with a partner to draw pictures of things that contain the long vowel sounds *e*, *o*, or *u*.

Day 5

Complete the Sort

Whole Group/Independent

Paste in Place

Encourage children to sort their pictures by long *e*, *o*, or *u* vowel sounds. Then have them turn to page 149 in their Word Study Notebook and paste the pictures in the correct column for each vowel sound.

Play the Game

When children are finished, they may play the Birdhouse game. (See the Teacher Resource CD for the game board, spinner, and directions.)

Building Vocabulary

Show children the mule picture card, and ask them what other animal it looks like. Explain that a mule is the offspring of a male donkey and a female horse. A donkey is an animal that is like a horse but smaller and with longer ears.

ESL/ELL English Language Learners

Review the picture names with children. Pay special attention to the words that contain diphthongs, making sure children are able to properly pronounce the words.

Teacher Tip

Encourage children to brainstorm individually or in small groups to suggest additional words that have the long vowels *e*, *o*, or *u*. Have children write their suggestions on the chalkboard and read them aloud to one another.

Long Vowels a, e, i, o, u

Objectives

- To identify long vowels *a*, *e*, *i*, *o*, and *u*
- To identify and sort picture names with long vowels *a*, *e*, *i*, *o*, or *u*

Materials

 Big Book of Rhymes, Level A, "I Wonder," page 75

 Teacher Resource CD, Level A

 Word Study Notebook, Level A, pages 151–154

 Words Their Way Library, Level A, *Cat's Trip*

 Teacher Resource CD, Level A, Pond Hop Game

Pictures

ā	ē	ī	ō	ū
wave	sleep	twine	goat	mule
skate	leaf	bike	road	suit
bake	jeans	vine	coat	June
cape	bean	smile	bone	cube

Day 1 Introduce the Sort

Whole Group

Read a Rhyme: "I Wonder"

Introduce long *a*, *e*, *i*, *o*, and *u* vowel sounds by reading the poem "I Wonder." After several readings, emphasize words that contain long *a*, *e*, *i*, *o*, or *u* vowel sounds. (*do, sleep, weep, fake, smile, while, goal, find, clue, those, true*) Ask children to identify the vowel sound in each word that you emphasize. Read the poem again, omitting the last word of each line, and have children provide the missing word.

Introduce Picture Sort
Long Vowel *a, e, i, o, u*

Whole Group

Print and cut apart the picture cards for Sort 38 from the Teacher Resource CD. Introduce the pictures, and define in context picture names that may be unfamiliar to children, such as *wave, skate, twine,* and *smile.* Then demonstrate for children how to sort the pictures by long *a*, *e*, *i*, *o*, and *u* vowel sounds. Ask children to describe how the pictures in each column are alike.

Day 2 Practice the Sort

Whole Group/Independent/Partner

You may want to begin Days 2–5 by rereading the rhyme from Day 1. Then review the previous day's sort demonstration. Help children remove page 151 from their Word Study Notebook and cut apart the cards.

Have children work independently or with a partner to say the name of each picture and, using the grid on page 153 in their Word Study Notebook, sort the cards by their long vowel sound.

> **Alternative Sort: What Can June Do?**
> When children are comfortable with this week's sort, tell them that June is not only the name of a month, but also a girl's name. Have children sort the cards into two categories—things that tell something that June could do and things that don't. Have children read the picture names aloud and give reasons why they sorted as they did.

Day 3 — Find Words in Context

Whole Group /Independent/Partner

Have children re-sort their cards. Then read the book *Cat's Trip* with children. Have children listen for and identify any words that include the long vowel sound *a, e, i, o,* or *u.*

Have children look through their cards to find pictures that match words in the text. Then have them find other words in the story that include a long *a, e, i, o,* or *u* vowel sound.

Day 4 — Apply the Skill

Independent/Partner

Have children sort their cards again. Then have children turn to page 154 in their Word Study Notebook. Read aloud the directions, and encourage children to work independently or with a partner to draw pictures of things that contain one of the long vowel sounds *a, e, i, o,* or *u.*

Day 5 — Complete the Sort

Whole Group/Independent

Paste in Place

Encourage children to sort their pictures by long *a, e, i, o,* and *u* vowel sounds. Then have them turn to page 153 in their Word Study Notebook and paste the pictures in the correct column for each vowel sound.

Play the Game

When children are finished, they may play the Pond Hop game. (See the Teacher Resource CD for the game board, playing cards, and directions.)

Building Vocabulary

Choose *wave, skate, bike,* or *smile* to review that a word can name both an object and an action. Say a sentence using one of the words as a noun. Have children make more sentences using the word as a noun. Then model how to make sentences using the word as a verb.

ESL/ELL English Language Learners

Review the pictures and words with children. Emphasize action words that contain long vowels (*wave, sleep, smile,* and so on) by acting out the motions associated with each word. Have children mimic your actions as they pronounce the action words.

Teacher Tip

Before children paste their picture cards into their Word Study Notebook, invite them to work with a partner to perform a "No Peeking" sort. Have one partner call out the name of each picture card while keeping the card hidden from the other partner. The other partner must use the sound of the word to decide which column on page 153 the card belongs in.

 ## Spell Check 6

After completing Sorts 36–38, you may want to administer Spell Check 6 in the Word Study Notebook on page 160. See page 19 for instructions on assessment.